Managing Translation Services

TOPICS IN TRANSLATION
Series Editors: Susan Bassnett, *University of Warwick, UK*
Edwin Gentzler, *University of Massachusetts, Amherst, USA*
Editor for Translation in the Commercial Environment:
Geoffrey Samuelsson-Brown, University of Surrey, UK

Other Books in the Series

For more details of these or any other of our publications, please contact:
Multilingual Matters, Frankfurt Lodge, Clevedon Hall,
Victoria Road, Clevedon, BS21 7HH, England
http://www.multilingual-matters.com

TOPICS IN TRANSLATION 32
Editor for Translation in the Commercial Environment:
Geoffrey Samuelsson-Brown, *University of Surrey*

Managing Translation Services

Geoffrey Samuelsson-Brown

MULTILINGUAL MATTERS LTD
Clevedon • Buffalo • Toronto

Library of Congress Cataloging in Publication Data
Samuelsson-Brown, Geoffrey
Managing Translation Services/Geoffrey Samuelsson-Brown.
Topics in Translation: 32
Includes bibliographical references and index.
1. Translating services. 2. Samuelsson-Brown, Geoffrey. I. Title. II. Series.
P306.94.S36 2006
418' .020285–dc22   2006011070

British Library Cataloguing in Publication Data
A catalogue entry for this book is available from the British Library.

ISBN 1-85359-914-X / EAN 978-1-85359-914-9 (hbk)
ISBN 1-85359-913-1 / EAN 978-1-85359-913-2 (pbk)

Multilingual Matters Ltd
UK: Frankfurt Lodge, Clevedon Hall, Victoria Road, Clevedon BS21 7HH.
USA: UTP, 2250 Military Road, Tonawanda, NY 14150, USA.
Canada: UTP, 5201 Dufferin Street, North York, Ontario M3H 5T8, Canada.

Typeset by Archetype-IT Ltd (http://www.archetype-it.com).
Printed and bound in Great Britain by the Cromwell Press Ltd.

Contents

List of Figures

Foreword

Now that I have gained years of experience and have burned my fingers on a number of occasions I have reflected on what I might have done differently. Success in any endeavour is the result of grasping opportunities as they arise and making the best of them. How you can achieve this can be the result of having an innate sense of what is right and what is wrong, listening to the advice of others and continuously developing your skills.

What skills you develop first is difficult to say but I would suggest that if you plan to develop and manage a translation company, or any enterprise for that matter, it is paramount to have a number of basic business skills. My own development started with being a freelance translator, learning business skills the hard way and, quite a few years later, 'going back to school' to consolidate my skills and improve them through formal education. Over a six year period I gained a Certificate in Management, a Professional Diploma in Management and, finally, a Degree of Master of Business Administration. Ideally I should have done this before making the transition from being a freelance to starting a translation company but life is seldom so ordered.

In addition to gaining invaluable skills, life-long learning (in a formal and structured manner) provides wonderful opportunities for making business contacts with people in all sorts of companies and organisations. It is through these contacts that you will grow your own business and learn about other businesses.

I would urge any freelance translator considering taking the plunge into the crocodile pool of business to develop business skills as quickly as possible. It is my endeavour with this book to offer useful words of advice that can be invaluable to the fledgling entrepreneur.

Dedication

This book is dedicated to my friend and contemporary Gordon Clark. While I had received my first introduction to word processors in the late 1970s when working as technical editor and translator for the Volvo Car Corporation in Sweden, it was Gordon who became my IT guide and mentor when I took the plunge and became a freelance translator in the UK in the 1980s.

IT, at least where freelance translation is concerned, was very new at the time but Gordon supported and encouraged my IT awareness when I purchased my very first word processor at a price that seemed a considerable financial risk at the time. However, I quickly learned about competitiveness and how the investment in what now seems very primitive equipment gave me real competitive advantage and allowed me gain the initial all-important customers on which to grow my business.

Our professional paths have diverged and Gordon has developed from selling word processing machines and other office equipment to becoming a European sales executive for a major IT company. Our friendship has developed over the years and I am indebted to Gordon for taking the time to provide a critical appraisal of this book.

Preface

This book provides a complement to *A Practical Guide for Translators* and looks at setting up and managing a translation enterprise. What is equally important is that it endeavours to identify and discuss issues such as what you want to get out of your business in the long term and how you might profitably dispose of your business when you feel it is time to make your exit.

The use of he/him/his in this book is purely a practical consideration and does not imply any gender discrimination on my part.

Moving from being a single practitioner to engaging other resources is often a natural progression for many freelance translators in response to being asked by customers about translating from or into languages in addition those in which the individual is competent. Educational bodies who teach languages and translation are beginning to offer translation services to a limited degree but few have yet to make a significant impact on the provision of commercial translation services.

My own experience covers working as a technical translator/editor for a major automotive company in Sweden and later at a research association in the UK as a senior project engineer. This was followed by a period as a freelance translator from which I progressed to developing a translation company that eventually had 15 employees and an extensive database of freelance translators and which I eventually sold. Since then I have taught translation studies to undergraduate and postgraduate students while maintaining my translation skills by accepting freelance translation and editing assignments.

It is probable that you already have some experience of translation in a commercial environment either as a staff translator or as a freelance working for agencies. For one reason or other you will have decided that you want to develop as a translation organisation and offer a range of languages and services in addition to those in which you yourself are qualified. It may sound a little blasé but recruiting freelance translators to work for you is easier than getting customers to whom you can market your services.

You may also have worked in a marketing and sales capacity for a translation organisation and, on the basis of your accumulated skills and experience, have decided to branch out on your own. A successful translation team combines a range of talents as illustrated in the following skills clusters.

Figure 1.   Principal skills required for managing translation services

This book deals primarily with managing what are generally referred to as technical, commercial and legal translation services and other added value services associated with translation and documentation.

Apart from business practices related principally to translation production and management this book contains sections on quality management that will facilitate the preparation of the necessary quality policy, procedures and instructions and allow the organisation to seek accreditation to the ISO 9001:2000 quality standard. Examples are also given of forms that can be used in managing a translation company. Research shows that only a small proportion of translation companies are accredited to this standard and, although I have never been asked for evidence of having achieved ISO 9001 accreditation, the fact that this is stated on your letterhead demonstrates evidence of your commitment to quality. At the time of writing the compilation of a European standard was in progress under the designation prEN 15038. More about this later in the book.

Research by the author[1] shows how few embryonic businesses have any sort of business plan apart from the notion of selling a product or service and, usually, making a profit.

The elements of a business plan will include the following short to medium-term considerations:

- Product and Services Development.
- Financial Plan – terms of business, profit and loss forecast, cashflow forecast.
- Resources Plan – physical resources, human resources, outsourcing.
- Marketing and Sales Plan.
- Quality Management.

A business plan will be essential if you intend seeking outside financial support from your bank or investors. At a later stage, it will also contain a confidential exit strategy for when you plan to dispose of your business or if you are approached by a prospective purchaser.

One of the biggest issues you will have to deal with is recruiting and retaining staff. Getting the right person for the job is crucial especially since engaging your first employee represents a major investment on your behalf.

A few years ago, The Chartered Institute of Personnel and Development (CIPD) asked 10,000 organisations to work out what it costs them every time someone leaves an organisation. The average cost of payroll and personnel time, recruitment, interview time, placement fees, training, 'unproductive' time, induction and loss in customer service and satisfaction came out at £3,456 for each person! And skills shortages mean it's going up all the time.

Technological change

Developments in technology mean that any reference to its application quickly becomes outdated. During my own career as a translator I have gone from writing my translations out by hand which were then copy-typed by a proficient copy-typist, through dictating translations which were then transcribed by an audio typist (or two during peak production periods), to working directly on a word processor and then progressing to today's technological wizardry.

Since technology changes so quickly that I have steered clear of discussing specific software and hardware tools. Obviously there is some commonality of word processing

---

1. Samuelsson-Brown, G.F. (2001) *Skills Auditing in Small to Medium-sized Enterprises*. MBA management research.

and other packages but the technology used to project-manage translation production is often tailor-made for the organisation that uses it. This is naturally the case when translations are offered or auctioned on-line.

Getting the balance right

The growing tensions between life and work are hitting us hard – as organisations and as individuals. It's clear that the old ways of working are simply not flexible enough to meet the pressures on people's time, the skills shortage, the changing balance of the population and the demands of customers. Something has to give – and in most organisations, it's people.

Absenteeism and sick leave are sometimes the last resort for people who have to care for children or aging parents. Employers are finding it hard to recruit and retain people and the cost of losing staff is high – perhaps up to 40% of yearly profits (research by the Hay Group – quoted on the 'Employers for Work–Life Balance' website). Just as damaging is the gradual wearing away of motivation and loyalty – two vital ingredients for meeting rising customer expectations.

Organisations know they have to tackle work-life balance. Legislation is designed to tackle specific issues such as flexible working arrangements for parents. But the fact is, everyone needs work–life balance, whatever their age or situation.

Running a translation organisation offers a great deal of flexibility if resources are appropriately managed. There is a high degree of inter-dependency between most translation organisations and their principal production resource – freelance translators. These translators have the option of accepting or rejecting assignments thereby managing their own work-life balance. While electronic project management has become inevitable there is the risk that it de-personalises the entire production process.

Translators have nearly always worked in isolation – usually by choice. The same applies to some degree to the relationship between the translation organisation and its customers. My own experience is that a working relationship can be developed over the phone but meeting a customer face-to-face, and not necessarily because there is a particular project to discuss, is invaluable.

When I first started doing translations it was on the invitation from an agency while I was working as a staff translator/technical editor in Sweden. At that time I wrote out my translations by hand at the rate of about 250 words an hour and did the translations in the evening after my normal daytime work. These were submitted for copy typing and sent back to me for checking after which any changes were made and hard copy was submitted to the client. I eventually progressed to dictating my translations but the procedure for production and delivery remained much the same.

By the mid-1980s I purchased my first PC having gone through the intermediate stage of using a word processor with its own dedicated software that needed to be loaded each time the computer was used. I felt that I was really at the forefront of technology when the word processor I used could store translations on floppy discs – 8″ double-density, double-sided discs with a storage capacity of 586 kb! I can now store 500 times this amount on a memory stick that I used for making backups of work in progress. What we now take for granted would have seemed difficult to believe at the time – how could we manage now without email and the Internet?

Globalisation has meant that a translation organisation can use resources world-wide and bypass many of the prejudices incurred through cross-border commerce. The fact that assignments can be posted on-line for translators to view and bid for has opened a broad market which, in many cases, has become more transparent. This reflects the enormous technological changes that have occurred over the last 20 years or so. The balance here is to harmonise business efficiency with the appropriate level of personal contact with the translator and customer.

While I accept unreservedly that this book may be considered ethnocentric, I believe that what it contains can be of value in whatever country you are operating from. My experience has been gained primarily from working in the United Kingdom and in Sweden but has also been added to by endeavouring to understand the business cultures of daily life and companies in other countries with whom I have developed working relationships.

Geoffrey Samuelsson-Brown
Bracknell, April 2006

1 Introduction

Translation is usually taken to mean the production of a written version of a source text in one or more target languages. There is physical evidence of the process and it can be subjected to analytical and tangible quality control.

Interpreting on the other hand is providing oral translation of speech. It is usually delivered consecutively when the speaker pauses to allow the interpreter to render into the target language what has been said in the source language. Simultaneous interpreting occurs while the speaker of the source text is speaking and does not pause for the interpreter to interpret before continuing to speak. Interpreting is, by its very nature, transient unless recorded for later analysis.

Translation as a profession is underrated and underpaid. The general perception is that the ability to speak a foreign language immediately implies the ability to translate into that language, not from it, irrespective of the subject area. Not only does the translator need to have the command of at least one source language and a target language plus a subject knowledge in these languages, he needs the skills to use the IT tools that are indispensable for the elements of the work to be done.

Until the translation profession becomes regulated the perception held by many who commission translations will remain unchanged. Fortunately moves are in progress in the United Kingdom through the Institute of Linguists and the Institute of Translation and Interpreting to change this situation but this will take time. Until then translation will remain a cost-led industry and there is a significant risk that students will hesitate to embark on at least four years of study at university, and incur a significant student loan, when the rewards that the profession offers will not encourage students to make the necessary commitment.

A person who studies to be an accountant, for example, can be expected to earn in the region of £40,000 a year if employed by a firm of accountants (2005 figures before tax) after having gained a first degree and a further three years of paid work experience, professional development and passing qualifying examinations. A freelance translator working for translation agencies can expect to earn in the region of £30,000 a year (less business expenses and taxes) if fully occupied and this is likely to increase by no more than the rate of inflation throughout his career irrespective of professional development and whatever additional qualifications he gains. The trained accountant can expect far greater rewards.

The worrying trend is that the translation profession is becoming an anonymous, internet-based profession where there is very little personal contact between the freelance and work provider. Fees offered to freelances have declined significantly over the last few years and thus the volume of work a freelance needs to get through to generate an acceptable income has increased proportionately. The danger of this development is that corners will be cut and quality will suffer.

What then is the lone freelance translator to do if he wishes to progress beyond this level? The only answer is to work for direct customers or develop a translation company that depends on the use of freelance translators to provide the range of languages and subjects that are demanded by potential customers. What is discussed in the following is relevant to both categories.

Freelance translation, in itself, offers a great deal of flexibility since the freelance is able to decide on the amount of work he accepts and this is ideally suited to those who wish to work from home or what is often referred to as a SOHO (Small Office Home Office). There is also a high degree of mutual dependence between freelance and a translation company but there needs to be appropriate rewards since not many freelances are prepared to work just for the love of translating and low rates of payment offered for the work. What needs to be considered when working from home is whether your activities contravene your rent, leasehold or freehold conditions or covenants. You may be faced with a demand for business rates for that part of your home that is used for business purposes.

Setting up a translation business

A brief introduction to running a translation business is given in Chapter 4 of *A Practical Guide for Translators*[2] but this is directed principally at a business run by a single freelance translator. However, a quote it contains from the Open Business School is worth repeating.

> *Running a business can be a dangerous activity for you and for others – just ask any of the 170,000 businesses that cease trading each year. In fact it is estimated that one in three businesses cease trading within their first three years of life – and two in three within their first ten years. And yet, although you need a licence to drive a car or fly a plane, you need nothing but reckless nerve and a first customer to start a business.*

2.   Samuelsson-Brown, G.F. (2004) *A Practical Guide for Translators*. Multilingual Matters Ltd., Clevedon.

There are many books on setting up in business but, by their very nature, are written to consider business in general and not translation services in particular. A reading list is Chapter 11.

Summary of tasks for setting up a company

Before you start to write your business plan (Yes! you do need a business plan) you will need to consider what you would like to do, what initial steps you need to go through and what events will affect the process. What you will have at the end will hopefully be a robust business plan that defines SMART objectives – those which are Specific, Measurable, Realistic and Timed.

The plan also needs to include a forecast of income and expenditure and probable cashflow. It's all very well generating a turnover and submitting invoices but the most important thing is making sure you get paid and the money goes into the bank.

First of all consider the following checklists.

1. What are you going to call your organisation?

- This should reflect professionalism from the outset.
- It should give an indication of what your organisation does.
- It will probably be limited company (Ltd) registered for VAT – this engenders confidence among customers. See Section 3 below.

What you call your organisation is very important and should reflect the corporate image you wish to project. Above all, it must project professionalism. Look though the Yellow Pages, for example, in the section on Translators and Interpreters and consider which adverts project a professional image. 'Creatively swipe' ideas and produce an advert that will gain attention.

Whilst recognising your organisation's limitations there is no benefit to be gained in advertising them – consider instead what commercial and competitive advantages you can offer your potential customers. The fact that you may be starting your business from a SOHO is irrelevant since there is no stigma attached to this as used to be the case. Most businesses evolve from an individual's aspirations and dreams. Where you operate your business from is far less important than the corporate image you project and the quality of the services you provide. To take an example, HP – better known as HP Invent (formerly Hewlett Packard) – was started in a garage by a certain Mr Hewlett and a certain Mr Packard. There are simple and practical options available once you feel the need to move from a SOHO to office premises away from home.

There are restrictions on what you can call your organisation. In the United Kingdom, guidance on forming a limited company and any restrictions on what you can call it can

3

be obtained from Companies House. The website to visit is www.companies-house.gov.
uk.

2. Have you appointed an accountant?

- If you have decided to form a limited company you will need to appoint an accountant/auditor. He will be able to deal with the formalities of registering a company for you. You can do this as a 'one-man-band' with a single director and a company secretary. Rather than thinking 'one-man-band' think micro-company. A potential customer is interested in what you can offer and is less concerned how you do this initially.
- It is useful to have an accountant even if you set up a sole trader business since he will be able to advise you on how you can operate your business in a tax-efficient manner. Separating business income and expenditure from your private affairs can be difficult. What you might pay out for the services of an accountant is well spent since this allows you to do what you are good at and leaves dealing with the authorities to somebody with the appropriate skills.
- Your accountant will be able to advise you on any changes in legislation that you may not be aware of. He will also prompt you when you need to make submissions to the Inland Revenue and other authorities. You have to consider your priorities.

3. Inform the appropriate authorities that you intend starting up in business

While your accountant can do this for you, the responsibility for ensuring that this is done rests with you as a proprietor or director of a company.

- Inform the Inland Revenue that you intend starting a business and that you wish to register for tax purposes.
- Inform Customs and Excise that you wish to register for Value Added Tax purposes. Your annual turnover may initially be lower than the threshold level for obligatory registration but being registered will allow you to reclaim Value Added Tax on purchases on a quarterly basis rather than considering expenditure at the end of your financial year.

These are questions that you need to consider before you deal with practical issues such as office equipment, office telephone, fax and modem, advertising, marketing, professional indemnity insurance and office contents insurance.

4. Data protection

If you plan to compile a database containing information on freelance and other resources you will need to register with the Information Commissioner to comply with data protection legislation under the Data Protection Act 1998. The current registration fee (2006) is £35.00.

Beware of bogus organisations that offer registration services at inflated charges – check with your accountant.

The details of the relevant body in the United Kingdom are:

Information Commissioner's Office
Wycliffe House
Water Lane
Wilmslow
Cheshire SK9 5AF
Website: www.informationcommissioner.gov.uk.

5. What service do you plan to offer initially?

While many embryonic businesses have grand plans for what they want to achieve, you need to consider carefully what you can actually provide while being able to maintain the highest level of skills appropriate to what you are offering your potential customers. Quite simply, you need to learn to walk before you can run. It is no good offering 'All subjects in all languages' when what you can actually provide falls woefully short of this.

The following considers the practical issues:

Specialised services with a narrow scope	'All subjects in all languages'
Advantages	
You can remain within the scope of your own skills (linguistic and subject range) and be confident of the quality you can provide. Your marketing will be focused since you will be able to identify your target market more easily. This is a company that you can run on your own and work within your own limitations	Providing you have the resources your scope is virtually unlimited.

Specialised services with a narrow scope	'All subjects in all languages'
Limitations	
Most translation companies offer a range of the most common languages plus a broad subject range. As a consequence you will be at a competitive disadvantage if your scope is narrow.	It would be unwise to offer all subjects and languages unless you have a database of freelance or staff resources that can provide quality translations and appropriate subject knowledge. It is also unwise to accept work and then try and find the relevant resources.
Development potential	
Naturally you have the scope to extend your business to include a greater range of languages and subjects by engaging staff or freelance translators.	It is realistic to assume that any company will start in a modest and manageable way. Once the company's reputation has been established this can form the basis of further development and possible diversification.

6.   From where are you going to run your business?

SOHO	From rented/leased or purchased premises
Advantages	
You do not have to commute to work and you can work whatever hours you want. You can switch on your answering machine when you do not wish to take calls. There may be a small tax allowance when you do this to cover heating and lighting etc. (currently £630 per annum in the UK)	Your office will be separate from your home and this allows you to get away from the office at the end of the working day. Although working from home does not produce any less-professional results, the sense of working from a rented office may be unjustifiably viewed as being more professional by potential customers. You will be able to call on additional support that you may use only occasionally if you work from services offices.
Limitations	
It is difficult to escape from the office at times and, unless you have separate telephone lines for your business, there is a risk that business calls could encroach on your private life. This requires a level of discipline.	Having to commute to work with all its attendant difficulties and costs. Access may be restricted outside working hours. Office rent and other costs need to be paid and you will inevitably be tied to a rent or lease contract (if you do not purchase premises).

SOHO	From rented/leased or purchased premises
Development potential	
Working from home allows you to earn an income while developing resources in an organic and manageable way. i.e. responding to opportunities. This type of growth is less risky but financial rewards take less time to realise. It allows you to consider the significant step of moving from a SOHO to a larger office in a rational manner	Moving office with a number of staff requires careful and detailed planning. You need to consider how this will affect your staff in terms of location and commuting. You will also need to consider the level of disruption and recovery caused by moving.

What type of organisation?

The most important tasks before starting a business are to consider a number of fundamental issues that concern the type of business enterprise you want to set up and to prepare a business plan. These are interdependent but let's consider the business identity first even though this will be determined to a great extent by your business plan. The following table considers the two most common formats for an embryonic business in the United Kingdom and the issues you need to consider.

	Sole trader or partnership	Limited company
Credibility	The advantages and disadvantages of a sole trader business and a partnership in terms of credibility are similar and the formalities involved in setting up this type of enterprise are quite simple.	On the whole it is perceived that being registered as a limited company gives your organisation more credibility. The same applies to being registered for Value Added Tax.
Registering a business	Setting up as a sole trader is very easy and incurs the fewest formalities. All you need do is contact your tax inspector and the Contributions Agency. Setting up a partnership is just as simple since there is no requirement to have a written partnership agreement. While full of initial enthusiasm and boundless trust these virtues must be tempered with realism and you would be wise to get a solicitor to draw up a partnership agreement on how partners are to divide profits, workload, taxes and what happens when partners change.	You can start up a limited company from a clean sheet of paper but perhaps the easiest way is to buy a company 'off the shelf'. This means buying a company from a company formation agent that is already registered and then change the name of the company to what you want to call it. The latter assumes that the intended name is not already registered and that certain other criteria are met. Your accountant can do this for a reasonable fee and can deal with registration with the Companies Registration Office. Registering a limited company implies certain obligations including submitting an annual return, accounts and changes in the company's officers.

	Sole trader or partnership	Limited company
Financial liability	As a sole trader you are personally liable for all the money owed by your business – in other words, your liability is unlimited. Your own personal assets such as your house and its contents, and your car can be seized to pay your business debts. In the worst case you could be made bankrupt. The same applies to a partnership. There is an additional disadvantage that you are liable for your business partner's share of any debts. Unlike a limited company a sole trader or partner cannot shed unlimited liability.	As the name implies, the liability of a limited company is limited. The liability for debts of shareholders in the company is usually limited to the amount they paid for their shares in the first place. Personal assets can be taken into account only if the company has been trading fraudulently. If, however, when starting up in business and have no track record it is common for you as a director to be asked to provide a personal guarantee for a bank loan/overdraft, leasing agreement or other credit arrangements. This may take the form of a second mortgage or a charge against an asset. As the company becomes more established and has achieved a good credit rating, having to provide such guarantees can usually be avoided.
Accounts and tax	Accounts for a sole trader business or partnership need to show a true and fair picture of you business and there is no legal requirement for a specific format in which the account must be laid out. In their simplest form they show turnover, expenses and profit. One dilemma that could arise is separating personal finances from business finances. A sole trader or partnership does not need to get its accounts audited. It is however useful and not expensive to do so and it will also help in your dealings with your tax inspector. It is also useful if you want proof of income if you plan to take out a loan or mortgage. As a sole trader or partner you will pay taxes in arrears on profit in the previous year. These are paid in three instalments.	The form of accounts for a limited company is laid down by law and such accounts must be submitted to the Companies Registration Office. Members of the public can inspect them there or purchase a copy. This can be useful if you want to research the competition. Small companies can submit abbreviated accounts but the formalities that apply to limited companies are more extensive than for sole traders and partnerships. As a member of a limited company you will pay tax each month according to the PAYE system similar to any employee of a company. The company's profits will be subject to taxation to be paid nine months after the end of the accounting year.

Table 1. Types of organisation

Another form of registered company is a public limited company. The shares in a company that goes under this designation may be transferred freely to members of the public. The company's shares may be traded on the Stock Exchange if the company is listed but this applies only to large companies. This form of company is not usual when starting out in business as a translation organisation since it requires a given level of equity capital.

On the basis of the above it would seem appropriate to form a limited company. A limited company must have at least one director and a company secretary – a sole director cannot act as a secretary. Other issues will be considered in an outline business plan and it is possible that you will make a loss in the first year or two of operations. This is something you need to consider in your plan and will depend how it is structured and whether growth is planned to be organic or accelerated. Growth through acquisition is also a consideration but issues concerning this need the guidance and skills of an appropriate adviser.

2 Organisational Development

Write a business plan!

Not having a business plan for your organisation means that you have not looked at the long-term objectives of your business. Articulating your business plan on paper also helps focus your ideas and discuss them with fellow shareholders and stakeholders. It is surprising that a significant proportion of SMEs (small to medium-sized enterprises) have no written business plan. Research by the author showed that almost 1 in 5 companies admitted that they had no written business plan. A simple process that can be used as a basis for a business plan is to consider your objectives, look at where you are now, and how are you going to reach your objectives. This is referred to as organisational development. If you need to raise finance either by issuing shares or taking out a business loan you are not likely to be taken seriously unless you have a realistic business plan.

You may offer excellent services but if you cannot identify a market for them you should seriously consider the validity of your business venture. Let's assume that you plan to start off on your own and on a scale that will allow for organic growth. In this way the entry costs will be moderate and your cashflow requirement will not be demanding. This will allow you to make a living but if you want to extend your scope beyond this you will need to consider bringing in additional resources to service customer demands.

Don't forget to look at long-term issues. Imagine that you are applying for a job as a senior executive in a translation company. What salary and bonuses would you expect? What private healthcare and other provisions would you expect? What pension provisions would you expect your potential employer to offer? Why should you not expect similar rewards from your own company. After all, you are taking all the initial risks.

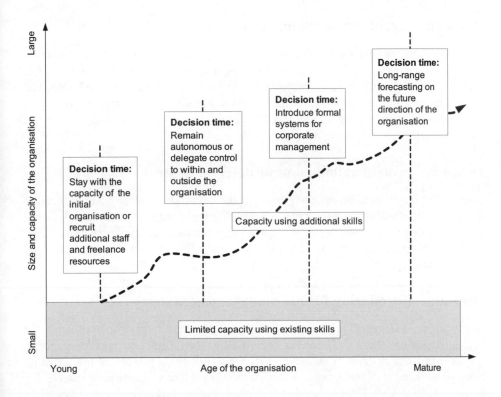

Figure 1. Stages in the growth of a translation organisation

Making the decisions

The nature of the profession allows you to assemble production resources fairly easily since there is a beneficial and mutual dependence between translation agencies and practitioners. The stages of growth from a 'one-man band' to translation organisation as illustrated above can be considered as a consequence of the following decisions.

Staying as a micro company

This is a fairly easy option to take since you will be responsible only for yourself. You make all the decisions (some with the guidance of your accountant etc) and you are not responsible for any other employees or freelances and your level of bureaucracy is limited.

Decision – recruiting additional staff

Once you have moved away from the idea of staying as a 'one-man-band' you are faced with decision of whether to cut down your own production as a translator or recruit additional staff. My own decision was to recruit an administrator who also had marketing and selling skills as the first step (nearly always the biggest one!). This was followed by recruiting an additional staff translator/quality controller and so the company grew.

Decision – remain autonomous or delegate control

There will come a time during the growth of the organisation when you will need to decide how this will affect you as the founder. You will need to release overall control and accept that the organisation will become departmentalised – production (including sub-contracting to freelances), administration (including project management), and business development.

Decision – introducing formal management systems

While an organisation is fairly small is it fairly easy for staff to have an overview of all that is happening. There will however come a time when formal systems for corporate management will need to be introduced. These will include job descriptions, quality management and staff regulations. Although this sound like a bureaucratic burden, it is better to have these in place rather that reacting to events. It is all important to consider what corporate image you wish to project.

Decision – long-range forecasting

Decisions, and particularly financial decisions, should not be based solely on extrapolating past data. This is where you will need to make an internal and external environmental assessment of potential events. How well will you be prepared if a key member of staff decides to leave? Are you prepared for external events that can impact your business and drive change? What will happen if a major customer is taken over and they no longer need your services. Just consider how IT has affected the way in which translators work over the past 10 years.

Your exit strategy (see Chapter 9) is part of long-range forecasting over which you have a great deal more control than external events. Forecasting is not just a matter of gathering information. You need to consider various scenarios that could occur. Forecasting leads to action even though this may only be confirming that what you are doing is correct and no change is necessary. C.W.MacMahon of the Bank of England is quoted as having said, '*No time is more usefully wasted as that spent guarding against disasters that do not in the event occur.*'

Skills for managing translation services

The principal skills required for managing translation services are as follows:

Skills element	Scope
Translation	Limited to the range of languages that you can offer with confidence and a guarantee of quality.
IT resources management	It is virtually impossible to run a business without a computer and email resources even at a very simple level.
Book keeping and accounts	Initially you may be happy enough to do this yourself but you will need to consider what is the best use of your income-generating time.
Marketing and sales	You may be a skilled translator but unless you can market your services it's a bit like smiling in the dark – you know you can do it but can your potential customers see you doing it? Consider how best you can market your business.
Project management	Translations that contain a single file require limited project management. However, it is not uncommon for a translation project to contain a large number of files in a range of languages that require careful project management.
Human resources management	Human resources are indispensable to your organisation and its success will depend on how well you manage these resources.
General administration	Consider administration as the oil that lubricates your organisation. Without it your organisation will grind to a halt.
Quality management	This seems to be a sensitive issue among translators and brings to mind issues such as criticism. If criticism is constructive it is valuable and should be accepted as part of continuous learning. If it is not constructive it can be rejected and reinforces your opinion that you were correct.

Figure 3. Elements of your organisation

Making the transition from single practitioner

When you go on a journey there are usually certain factors that you need to consider before setting off. Let's assume that you are going by car. You'll need to know the following:

- What is your intended destination?
- When do you plan to get there?
- What time you plan to leave?

You'll also need certain resources for the journey:

- Fuel, oil, water, refreshment and possible breaks along the way.
- A route – either in your head or by referring to a map.

Or simply:

- Where do you want to get to?
- Where are you now?
- And how are going to get there?

Business development can be considered in much the same way and can be illustrated in the following seven steps:

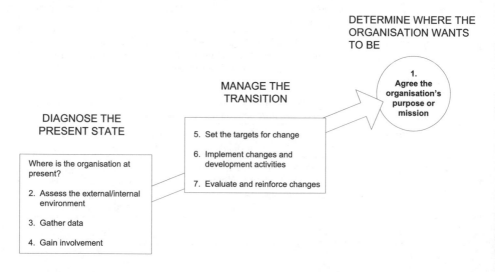

Figure 4.   Stages of business development

Let's go through the stages one at a time and build some structure for our business plan.

Determine where the organisation wants to be

Stage 1. Agree the organisation's purpose or mission

You need to consider where you want the organisation to be in, say, two year's time. This is quite a long-term perspective when starting out in business since it could change rapidly during the initial phase of its growth. Your business plan will not be set in stone and will be subject to regular reviews and amendments on the basis of experience. These reviews will be more frequent while the business is in the early stages of growth. Your bank manager will have a vested interest in your success and will often work together with you on these reviews. Most of the major banks offer useful business advice and regular reviews of you progress.

A lot of what are termed 'mission statements' are usually quite bland and pretentious but you need to make a start somewhere. Let's go with the following:

> XYZ Translation Ltd delivers translation and documentation services in a range of languages to industry and commerce. Its services are provided by qualified translators and project managers all of whom have skills that meet the organisation's strict quality requirements.

We've now decided broadly what we want to do and to whom our services will be directed. We now need to look at where we are starting from.

Diagnose the present state

Stage 2. Assessing the external/internal environment

During this process you need to consider what external forces can have an effect on your organisation. These include customers, suppliers of goods, suppliers of services (including freelances), authorities (local and central government), competitors and other market forces. These are often considered by using what is referred to a STEP analysis (or PEST analysis if you are a pessimist) which looks at Socio-cultural, Technological, Economic and Political/legal factors that can influence the development of your organisation. You need to consider which of these have an immediate effect when starting your organisation and what are likely to affect the organisation in the future – such issues include taxation and the level of resources to achieve your corporate objectives. See Table 3 below.

During the initial stage of growth it is fairly easy to assess the internal environment – this is the place where you work and your resources.

Stage 3. Gathering data

You will need to gather data on your intended market so that you can carry out the necessary marketing to potential customers. How you do your research depends on the types of companies you want to target and how you want to grow. You may decide to grow organically (grasping opportunities as they arise) or mechanically (through active marketing and selling).

You also need to look at what your competition is doing. You can do a lot of research by looking at websites but this will not provide information on what rates competing organisations charge. While the Institute of Translation and Interpreting carries out surveys of rates charged by freelances there is no information on what translation agencies and companies charge.

My own experience indicates that it useful to engage an independent consultant to research this information for you since he can be honest and state that he is carrying out independent research on behalf of a customer who wishes to commission translations. You can provide him with examples of typical assignments (while respecting confidentiality) so that he in turn can ask for pricing from a sample of translation agencies. This will provide you with reasonable benchmark prices on which you can base your own services. The cost of engaging a consultant can be recouped by charging realistic but competitive prices rather than guessing and starting off too low. You can always reduce prices but it is very difficult to raise prices once you have made your bid. Don't sell yourself or your organisation too cheaply.

Stage 4. Gaining involvement

To do this you need to look at the stakeholders in your organisation and the influence they may exert on your activities. Some are peripheral whereas others are central.

Stakeholder	Influence or interest
Your bank or other source of finance	You may need initial finance in the form or a loan or overdraft. The provider of finance obviously has an interest in the success of your organisation so that any loan or overdraft can be redeemed or repaid, and that you will continue to use their services. Your bank is often required as a reference when opening a credit account with suppliers.

Stakeholder	Influence or interest
Central and local government (including the EU)	Influences and interests are many. You are required to comply with legislation issued by central government as well as directives issued by the EU. If you operate from commercial premises you will need to pay business rates to your local authority. Both levels of government can also be useful sources of information.
Customers	Customers depend on you for the services you provide and, when you have built up a good working relationship, can offer a source of mutually-beneficial training and expertise improvement.
Your staff and business partners	Unless you continue to operate as a 'one-man-band' there will be a mutual dependence on both these stakeholders. Your organisation will offer a source of work and employment in return for added-value services that are commercially attractive.
Your shareholders	Shareholders are obviously interested in the success of your organisation and a yield on their investment. You may be the only shareholder but the sentiment remains the same
Suppliers of goods and services (including freelance translators and interpreters)	You depend on the services that suppliers provide and, when you have built up a good working relationship, can offer a source of mutually-beneficial training and expertise improvement as in the case of customers. Some people would argue that freelances who offer their services should be fully trained. I would argue that training is a life-long endeavour. I do not advocate that you should provide training on software such as MS Word but that freelances should be fully briefed on non-standard requirements. If you plan to work on a major project it can be an advantage to invite the translators you intend engaging for a meeting at your premises (or book a meeting room at a nearby hotel if your premises are too small) to preview the project and collectively discuss requirements. The opportunities that freelances get of meeting agencies are few and far between and should be grasped to consolidate working relationships and share experiences.
Inland Revenue	The influence of the Inland Revenue is very powerful and could break your organisation if you do not comply with your responsibilities. The Revenue can also be very helpful by providing useful information and advice – particularly to those starting up in business.
Customs and Excise	For the most part you will be concerned with Customs and Excise if you are registered for Value Added Tax. (At the beginning of 2005, the threshold for VAT threshold in the United Kingdom was an annual turnover of £58,000). This means that if you charge less VAT on your services than you pay for goods and services, you will be able to reclaim the difference when you make out you quarterly return. If your business is not registered for VAT you will have to wait until your annual accounts are prepared. Since it is relatively simple to calculate VAT, especially when you computerise your book-keeping and accounts, it is worth registering since your organisation is often viewed as being more serious and substantial in this case. It also means that the VAT charged remains in your account until you make your quarterly return.

Stakeholder	Influence or interest
Professional organisations such as the Institute of Translation and Interpreting	Since translation remains an unregulated profession, there is no requirement to be a member of professional institutions. Membership is however viewed as benchmark of the skills offered by the individual translator or corporate member. The Institute of Linguists is now introducing chartered status for its members. This and similar moves by Institute of Translation and Interpreting such as monitoring continuous personal development can only enhance the status of the profession and bring to it the higher level of recognition it deserves.

Table 2.   Stakeholders in your organisation

Gaining the involvement of some of these is vital to the success of your enterprise and they will need to be informed of its progress. Some whom you think are only there to take a share of your hard-earned income (Inland Revenue etc.) can be extremely helpful and arrange free seminars to assist enterprises that are just getting started. Most banks now offer a start-up package, including a model business plan to new business customers.

Gaining and maintaining the involvement of your staff, partners, shareholders and suppliers of goods and services, not least freelances, is vital unless you intend staying a 'one-man band'.

Managing the transition

A successful freelance working full time for agencies is probably capable for generating an annual turnover of around £30,000 based on working 10.5 months a year and 8 hours a day. Allowing for operating expenses, this will provide a pre-tax profit (or salary) of around £20,000. Most freelances probably work longer hours but it is better to be realistic than have inflated expectations.

Don't imagine that your time will be spent solely on translation production. If I were to make a rough analysis of my average working month of 22 possible working days I would get the following:

Task or item to which time is accounted	Time spent on the task
Translation including project management, research, draft translation, proof reading and editing, resolving queries and administration	Fourteen and a half days
Office administration including filing, invoicing and checking that invoices get paid and, if not, taking measures to ensure payment, purchasing and correspondence. Tax issues, book-keeping, annual accounts and auditing are dealt with by my accountant	Two days

Task or item to which time is accounted	Time spent on the task
External activities such as networking and marketing. Dealing with sales calls that are directed at me or my business.	One day
Continuous personal development. A lot of continuous personal development is opportunistic in response to the demand of the task you undertake as part of your work – learning new aspects of software etc.	Two days
Public or other holidays (say 21 days leave and 7 days public holidays)	Two and a half

My average monthly output for these fourteen and a half effective days is, on average, around 34,000 words. If this is spread out over effective working days of 8 working hours (8 x 50 minutes in reality), my effective hourly production rate is roughly 300 words an hour. This may not seem a lot but it may be worth considering that to expect to work undisturbed on translation eight hours a day, five days a week, is quite unrealistic. There may also be times when you are physically or mentally unable to work – how do you take account of such eventualities as a freelance? There are also fluctuations in work loads that need to be considered.

Stage 5. Setting the targets for change

Setting targets for change is difficult but, unless targets are set and you do not apply the appropriate resources, you will not be able to progress from being a 'one-man band'. Let's look at targets – these are hypothetical to some degree but without targets there is nothing to strive towards nor measure against.

While on the subject of targets or objectives, there's the useful acronym we've mentioned already. Make sure your objectives are SMART as explained in the following.

Objective	Purpose
Specific	Define what you plan to achieve during the life of the business plan. All business plans are subject to regular review and objectives are therefore revised as a consequence. A specific objective might be to achieve a production turnover of 100,000 words a month.
Measurable	All objectives need to be measurable to assess the level of success. Consequently, a production turnover of 100,000 words is tangible and can be measured.
Achievable	There is no point in setting an objective if it is not achievable. For example, to be achievable you will need to have or be able to develop the resources to translate, say, 100,000 words a month.

Objective	Purpose
Realistic	An objective needs to be realistic if it is to be achieved. It is unrealistic to try and enter a particular market if the entry barriers are insurmountable.
Timed	A time limit for achieving an objective needs to be set. For example, the financial viability of your business plan may depend on achieving a turnover of, say, £15,000 a month within six months of starting your business.

Three criteria are useful in this regard.

1. Considering the services you plan to offer (and the necessary skills).
2. Marketing to create an awareness of the services you provide.
3. Developing 'in-house' resources to manage the services you offer.

These are considered in the following.

What services do you plan to offer?

The term services is used even though all services have a product content and all products have a service content. The following are obvious categories but there is often an overlap between them. You also need to consider what languages you plan to offer. If you refer to Figure 3 above you will remember that there are two fundamental choices – stay within the limitation of the resources you have or expand by engaging additional resources. This book is based on the assumption that your organisation will grow by using additional resources – office staff and freelances. You may consider acquisition as a way to grow but this is not usually on the minds of people in a start-up phase.

It is all too easy to offer the world and worry about sourcing skills when demand

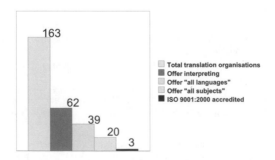

Figure 5. Sample analysis of translation organisations

arises. Research on a random sample of 163 translation organisations on the basis of their advertising claims reveals some interesting facts.

- Almost 40% offer interpreting as well as translation services – the two go hand in hand.
- Close on 25% of the advertisers offer translations in all languages. One company offered 'All European and World languages' (Are not European languages World languages?). Others quoted that they covered a large range of languages with one advertiser stating specifically that it offered translations in 140 languages.
- Approximately 1 company in 8 offers translations in all subjects.
- Only 3 companies in the survey (less than 2%) advertised that they held accreditation to ISO 9001:2000.

These claims may sound impressive but are they credible? If you plan to offer all the languages and subjects that your customers demand you need to make sure that you have the resources available and are able to provide the level of quality that is appropriate. There are cases where you will need to rely implicitly on your translators and that your customer is fully aware of the scope of the services you offer. It is worth repeating that you should politely decline assignments if you know you are unable to provide the resources.

Translation

The basic elements of the translation process can be illustrated in many ways depending on the complexity of the project but the following can be used as a starting point.

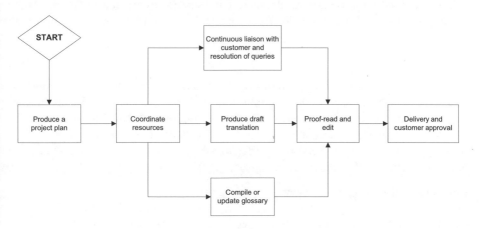

Figure 6. Elements of the translation process

General translations for information purposes

The usual assumption is that, unless a specific purpose is specified by the customer, a translation is provided for information purposes only. Always ask what the intended purpose of the translation is since the customer may not have considered this or be aware that translations can be presented in different ways.

The quality criterion for this type of translation is that it should be correct.

Specialised translations

The term 'specialised translation' implies that the translator will need to have an adequate knowledge of a particular discipline in addition to being a qualified translator. I use the term specialised translation rather than technical or legal. While dictionaries are useful there is no substitute for detailed subject knowledge as well as knowing and understanding the appropriate terminology in the target language.

The quality criterion for this type of translation is that it should be correct in terms of translation and the use of specialised terminology.

Translations for publication in one form or another

This often includes specialised translations but there are greater demands on the way in which the translation is presented. The translator is being asked more and more to produce the translation in a particular format using a document template or a particular software format such as PowerPoint and PageMaker.

This type of translation often needs to be culturally-adapted for a particular market. The process is often referred to as 'localisation' and may include the translation of websites plus the use of formats such as HTML.

The criterion for this type of translation is that it should be correct terms of translation and the use of specialised terminology, and that the layout and presentation comply with customer requirements.

Certified translations

Some translations required for legal or official purposes need to be certified or authorised. This means, in essence, that the translator makes a translation and then attaches a statement or letter stating that he is competent to make a certified translation of the relevant documents. An example of a certification letter is shown on page 23. The acceptance of such certification may differ in various countries. More details can be found in 'A Practical Guide for Translators'.

Checking and editing as a service

This requirement can arise when a customer is not satisfied with an existing translation services provider as a result of comments from an end user. You may be asked to provide an assessment of and report on work that has been done. This is

GSB consulting ltd.

100 Northcott, Bracknell, Berkshire RG12 7WS, United Kingdom ● Web site: www.gsbconsulting.co.uk ● Email: info@gsbconsulting.co.uk
● Tel: +44 (0)1344 319570 ● Fax: +44 (0)1344 319571 ● Mobile: +44 (0)771 8900431 ● Registered number: 3862171 ● VAT No: GB 731 7514 45

To whom it may concern

CERTIFICATION

I, the undersigned, Geoffrey Francis Samuelsson-Brown, DipTrans IoL, Fellow of the Institute of Linguists, Fellow of the Institute of Translation and Interpreting, and Member of the Swedish Association of Professional Translators, having a knowledge of the Swedish and English languages, declare that the translations of the attached documents from Swedish into English are, to the best of my knowledge and belief, are true and faithful renderings of the faxed Swedish language documents.

While every effort has been made to ensure accuracy in translation, the original Swedish documents take precedence over the translations in the event of any dispute concerning interpretation.

Attachments (with each page identified by the company stamp and my initials)

Translations from Swedish into English (3 pages)

Swedish certificate of registration (1 page)

Swedish degree certificate (2 pages)

Dated Bracknell, 21 December 2004

(Signature)

Geoffrey Samuelsson-Brown
MBA FIL FITI DipTrans DipMgmt

Certificate No: 11078

probably not a service that you would advertise although this could offer a competitive advantage.

This may also arise when a well-meaning customer has made a translation and asks you to 'just check through it'. The customer is under the illusion that he is saving time and money but the end result is seldom as good as that which could have been achieved by a translator making a translation in the first place. Experience shows that 'just checking' usually takes longer than translation since it is often necessary to make a mental translation back into the source language to understand what the writer had intended and then make a retranslation into the target language.

There are also the very professional companies who want to ensure that the quality of language used in their publications is of the highest level. A good example of this is an international company that uses English as a corporate language. The level of English spoken for day-to-day usage may be adequate for the purpose but not necessarily for publication. It then becomes the job of the translator/editor to ensure that the text is editing according to an agreed corporate style and can then be successfully translated into other languages in corporate publications. The translator/editor often has the task of clarifying what was intended before there is a chance of any ambiguities being mistranslated.

Interpreting

Since the majority of interpreters work independently, translation companies maintain a list of interpreters and act as an agency for such service providers as and when the demand arises. Interpreting is usually provided as an added-value element to written translation services.

Document engineering

This is a term that applies to the production and management of documentation and can include translation as part of services in the organisation's value chain. The basic elements of document engineering are illustrated in Figure 7.

Marketing to create an awareness of the services you provide

Marketing can be defined as identifying a customer need and satisfying that need so that both your organisation and the customer derive benefits. Selling is identifying the customer and convincing him that your organisation is the one to satisfy his needs.

Identifying potential customers or prospects is not easy. They are likely to be organisations that import or export goods and services or plan to do so. Marketing is opportunistic and there are several ways you can gain new customers:

- through passive marketing in directories such as the Yellow Pages

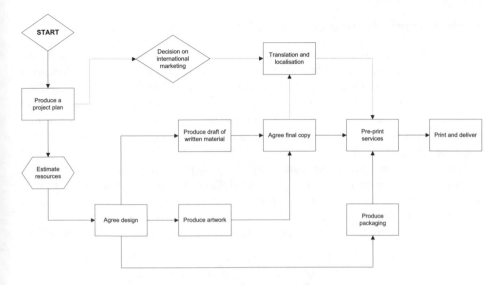

Figure 7. Elements of document engineering

- by providing a better service than an organisation's existing service provider
- as a result of being approached by an organisation that plans to develop in a new market and is not already using a translation services provider
- by being recommended or referred by existing customers
- through networking at events organised by various bodies such as chamber of commerce (such events normally require you to be a member)
- by getting as much publicity as possible through exposure in the press

Though entry barriers into the market in terms of equipment are fairly low since there is no major investment in stock and similar goods, it is not easy to break into a mature market. There are different market forces that can affect your organisation:

- organisations who are already working in the industry and who jockey for position among current competitors
- the threat of new entrants (this is where you come in!)
- the bargaining power of customers – translation services are cost-led unless you can offer unique skills and added-value
- the threat of substitute products or services (these may include free translations on-line but may also confirm the need for a professional human translator)
- the bargaining power of suppliers – the cost of service (and goods) you purchase from your suppliers (principally your freelance translators).

Stage 6. Implementing change and development activities

Probably the biggest step you will take as a 'one-man-band' is to take on an additional employee. Since your time is best spent doing what you are good at (translation) it is appropriate to engage somebody who can take over some of the administrative burdens. Releasing some of your time for more income-generating work will cover some or all of the costs of an additional person. Consider what your earning potential is per hour and whether it is better delegate (or subcontract) the tasks that you are less good at or you hate doing.

This person can work under your guidance and, presuming you have written an appropriate job description and recruited the right person, will have the skills to help you build the organisation. What the person's job title should be is difficult to decide but I would suggest Project Manager since this gives an appropriate status and can easily be identified by customers. Ideally the candidate would deal with the following tasks:

- Developing an initial database of freelance service providers (principally translators) to meet the demands of the market you plan to approach.
- Approaching prospects so that new business can be generated.
- Providing prospects with information about the organisation in the form of printed marketing material and reference to your website.
- Arranging appointments for you or the project manager to visit a potential customer.
- Project administration for the work you do (and the work done by freelance translators do).
- Book-keeping if this is to be done in-house.

As the organisation grows it may be necessary to take on additional staff. This development should be very carefully considered since each new employee means additional responsibility not least in financial terms. It is unlikely that your business will grow at a steady rate. You will therefore need to carry out 'what-if?' analyses so that you can cope with the ups and downs of the business cycle.

Stage 7. Evaluating and reinforcing changes

Initially and while you are still involved in all aspects of your developing organisation you will be aware of everything that is going on. You still need to evaluate and reinforce changes through regular reviews with the staff that you may have employed. This process becomes more complex as the organisation grows. It is also iterative and continuous.

This is not the end of the story since the procedure can be used when considering growth in future strategy reviews.

3   The Business Plan

What services resources do you plan to offer?

While many embryonic businesses have grand plans for what they want to achieve you need to consider carefully what you can actually provide while being able to maintain the highest level of skills appropriate to what you are offering your potential customers. Quite simply, you need to learn to walk before you can run.

All languages in all subjects?

It is no good offering 'all languages in all subjects' when what you can actually provide falls woefully short of this. As it is, I consider being able to translate 'all languages and all subjects' to be rather an inflated claim. Would the organisation making this claim actually be able to respond to the potential demand?

There are always dangers when attempting to grow too quickly. Growth can be quite sudden when major project presents itself and, while potential rewards are attractive, you need to ensure that the resources, both human and financial, you can call upon will support the project. While it may sound pessimistic it is always worth carrying out a 'what-if?' analysis of anything that is doubtful. Try and ensure that no more that 25% of your turnover comes from a single customer. This decision must be tempered by a risk analysis.

The following considers the practical issues:

Specialised services with a narrow scope	'All subjects in all languages'
Advantages	
You can remain within the scope of your own skills (linguistic and subject range) and be confident of the quality you can provide. Your marketing will be focussed since you will be able to identify your target market more easily. This is a company that you can run on your own and work within your own limitations.	Providing you have the resources your scope is virtually unlimited.
Limitations	
Most translation companies offer a range of the most common languages plus a broad subject range. As a consequence you will be at a competitive disadvantage if your scope is narrow.	It would be unwise to offer all subjects and languages unless you have a database of freelance or staff resources that can provide quality translations and appropriate subject knowledge. It is also unwise to accept work and then try and find the relevant resources.
Development potential	
Naturally you have the scope to extend your business to include a greater range of languages and subjects by engaging staff or freelance translators.	It is realistic to assume that any company will start in a modest and manageable way. Once the company's reputation has been established this can form the basis further development and possible diversification.

From where are you going to run your business?

SOHO	From rented premises
Advantages	
Your initial costs are small and may include converting a spare room for office use. About 10 m^2 would be enough to start with when you consider the space required for furniture, equipment and bookshelves. Reasonable expenses for this are usually tax deductible. You do not have to commute to work and you can work whatever hours you want. You can switch on your answering machine when you do not wish to take calls. There may be a small tax allowance when you do this to cover heating and lighting etc. (currently £600 per annum in the UK). Allowances are made for reasonable repairs but, if there is any doubt in your mind, contact your accountant.	Your office will be separate from your home and list allows you to get away from the office at the end of the working day. Although working from home does not produce any less-professional results, the sense of working from a rented office may be unjustifiably viewed as being more professional by potential customers. You will be able to call on additional support that you may use only occasionally if you work from services offices.

SOHO	From rented premises
Limitations	
It is difficult to escape from the office at times and, unless you have separate telephone lines for your business, there is a risk that business calls could encroach on your private life. This requires a level of discipline. It is tempting to charge your business for office rent for the area set aside for this purpose. If you do so, you will be subject to capital gains tax on the portion of the house when you sell it. You may risk violating your rent agreement or the covenants of your freehold or leasehold by using part of your home for commercial purposes.	Having to commute to work with all its attendant difficulties and costs. Access may be restricted outside normal working hours Office rent and other costs need to be paid and you will probably be tied to rent or lease contract.
Development potential	
Working from home allows you to earn an income while developing resources in an organic and manageable way. This type of growth is less risky but financial rewards take less time to realise. It allows you to consider the significant step of moving from a SOHO to a larger office in a rational manner.	Moving office with a number of staff requires careful and detailed planning. You need to consider how this will affect your staff in terms of location and commuting. You will also need to consider the level of disruption and recovery caused by moving.

Overview

There are several reasons for compiling a business plan:

- You are starting a new translation agency or company.
- You are preparing a presentation for a bank or investors when raising starting capital. This can be achieved through an overdraft facility, bank loan or investment by partners or shareholders. Consider what you might need to provide in terms of security if you have no real business track record.
- You are planning to expand and need additional working capital.

If you are considering starting a new business you need to decide what type of organisation you consider to be appropriate. In all cases you need to consider a number of fundamental questions:

- What is the purpose of the plan?
- What will finance be needed for?
- How much finance is required?
- How will finance be raised?
- Investment by owners and/or shareholders.

- Describe the business and analyse its intended markets.
- How do you plan to differentiate your organisation from the competition?
- Who will be the stakeholders?
- How will you establish the credibility of the organisation?
- What are the financial projections?
- What does an analysis of strengths, weaknesses, opportunities and threats (SWOT analysis) reveal?

Delegation and departmentalisation

By this stage you will probably have made the decision to employ additional staff. Even there may only be two of you in the organisation you will have delegated or share some of the tasks that you used to do on your own. While you have no departments as such it is worth thinking of the 'corporate image' you wish to project. It is seldom that customers visit you and, although visits should be encouraged when you feel comfortable with the prospect, most of your face-to-face contact with customers it at their premises. They are seldom particularly interested whether or not you have an impressive office. What is important is that you provide impressive services and appropriate security for customer information and documents.

Think along the lines of how you would like your organisation to be, say, in two years time and consider what departments would be appropriate. Each department will have its own plan that forms part of the overall business plan. In addition there should be a training plan to meet the needs of all departments.

It is vital that you project the appropriate professional image right from the start otherwise customers will view you as a low-cost, low-tech cottage industry. You will feel exploited and find it difficult to charge the fees that are appropriate to the level of services you provide.

Let's consider what departments (or sections if you're not yet comfortable with the use of the word departments) there will be in your organisation:

- Marketing and sales.
- Project management.
- Production and quality management.
- Purchasing goods and services.
- Business administration.

Each department will contribute to a Strategy Group that will look at business development in the long term. Each will have its objectives that will be part of the overall plan and will harmonise with those of the other departments.

Eventually your business plan will contain a number of departments each of which will contribute to the growth of the organisation. The following offers suggestions but obviously you will develop the organisation as you consider appropriate.

- Marketing and sales.
- Administration and project management.
- Production and quality control.
- Human resources.

Marketing and sales

The principal tasks of the Marketing and Sales Department are:

- Promotion of the organisation to ensure appropriate business development.
- Identification of future resources requirements.
- Identification of training requirements.
- Production of the organisation's Marketing and Sales Plan and contributing to the overall business plan.

A difficult issue is to determine the difference between marketing and sales. My understanding is as follows:

- Marketing is identifying a customer need and satisfying that need so that both you and the customer derive a benefit.
- Selling is convincing the potential customer that you are the best organisation to satisfy the need that has been identified.

Marketing and sales can be passive or active and is usually a combination of both. Passive marketing and sales are usually achieved in a number of ways with the objective of maintaining a presence and gaining exposure in front of potential customers. It is easy to spend lots on money on advertising and Yellow Pages and other directories provide passive exposure in relation to advertising costs. When approached I have always asked an enquirer how he found out about the organisation and the answer has usually been, ' . . . through the Yellow Pages'.

Beware of what turn out to be bogus directories and magazines that offer advertising space and the opportunity to write an article about your organisation. I have experienced buying advertising space and writing an article only to find out that when I have asked for a copy of the directory that the company supposedly producing the publication has disappeared from the face of the earth. There had been no intention to publish. Unless you know about or have seen the publication ask for a copy of a past issue or otherwise validate its existence. It is all too easy to spend money on advertising that produces no return.

Business cards are indispensable. Even though I pick up possibly half a dozen business cards when I go to a business event it is probably that most will not lead to immediate business. I always file these cards in a folder with plastic pockets designed for the purpose. When you are given a business card, don't just say thank you and stick it in your pocket. Take the time to read the information on it and, as a reminder of the event, write a few details and the date on the back of the card. This will also indicate to the person who gave you the card that you are genuinely interested and not just a polite collector. If people remember you there is the possibility of referrals to a third person.

The way in which technology has developed in recent years means that you can now include your website in your advertising. This can be kept updated at all times and is far more dynamic and informative than a glossy brochure that can be expensive to produce and becomes outdated quickly.

Identifying possible customers takes a lot of research and personal involvement but the potential rewards are obviously much greater than passive advertising. It is a hard discipline for a small organisation when what your really want to get on with the work in hand since this generates fairly immediate income. Set an objective of contacting say two prospects a day. This doesn't sound much but will probably take up an hour when you consider the time taken on research, data management and administration. The potential level of response will allow you to manage growth and the approach is far better than sending out a mass mailing where you might have difficulty in managing the response with your initial resources.

If you maintain this level of marketing you will approach in the region of 45 prospects a month. If you target your sales prospects it is not unreasonable to hope for at least a couple of new customers a month or 25 over a year. Add to this the potential enquiries you will receive through passive advertising and you will have a good customer base on which to grow your organisation.

Where to start?

It is worth trying to consider the difference between marketing and selling. To my mind, marketing is identifying a customer need and satisfying that need so that both parties derive benefits. Selling is advertising (in the broadest sense) and gaining a potential customer's attention or interest so that you can make an approach or he can contact you about providing services.

There are three principle ways in which you can gain new customers:

- Being in the right place at the right time when a customer has a particular need that is not already satisfied. This is serependipitous and cannot be controlled.
- Offering services that your competitors do not provide.
- Convincing a user of an existing supplier that you can offer something better and more cost-effective.

Identifying a potential customer is not easy. If you decide you want to target a particular industry sector you can use the Yellow Pages or one of the many directories that are published. Some of these are available in electronic format which will facilitate searching – you will however have to pay for such information in most cases. In the United Kingdom you can start with the Directory of UK Associations. Since this is fairly expensive (£190 in 2005) it may be worthwhile going to your public library and do your market research using their copy. This will allow you to research information in the industry sectors you wish to approach. It is also possible to buy address lists from various brokers. Only you can determine which approach is suitable for your business.

Since you need to manage your freelance resources and your customer base it seems appropriate to use software such as Microsoft Access to manage all the information. Ideally this should be structured so that the information is integrated.

Administration and project management

Administration is often viewed as the unglamorous part of an organisation but, without efficient administration and project management, the organisation would not function efficiently and could fall apart.

Administration staff provide the day-to-day interface with customers and is often the first contact that a potential customer has with the organisation. The quality of the customer interface sets the tone of the entire organisation and, as a consequence, staff who come in direct contact with customers and freelance suppliers must receive appropriate training and have a proper knowledge of what translation involves. This will ensure that staff can deal satisfactorily with enquiries from customers, inspire confidence, and allocate assignments to the freelance resources that have the relevant language skills and subject knowledge. Although it is necessary to work within the resources available any such enquiry can be an indication of resources that need developing.

The principal tasks of the Administration Department are:

- Providing a credible and professional interface with customers.
- Promoting the organisation to ensure appropriate business development.
- Coordinating existing resources and managing the freelance database to meet customer requirements.
- Maintaining the customer database.
- Project management.
- Book-keeping and accounts.
- Identifying future resources requirements.

- Identifying potential marketing opportunities and passing marketing intelligence to the marketing and sales department.
- Producing the organisation's Human Resources Plan and Financial Plan and contributing to the Marketing Plan and ultimately the Business Plan.

Customer enquiries and allocation of resources

Simple projects that involve a single file for translation from one source language to one target language can be handled using a work order form – an example is given in Appendix 5. More complex projects containing a large number of files can be tracked by setting up a file in Excel showing the various stages to completion and delivery.

Major projects that include various production phases and a range of languages are best handled by using project management software such as Microsoft Project. Such software is also beneficial when presenting a bid for translation work and demonstrating how you plan to do the work to meet detailed customer requirements and where one phase of the project may depend on the completion and approval of a previous phase.

A face-to-face meeting may not be required for a simple project. You should however take the opportunity to visit a customer since personal contact allows you to assess potential and the customer to put a face to the anonymity of telephone calls and emails. Meetings help to cement longer-term relationships and anticipate resource and training requirements.

File management

Let's look at a hypothetical job where a number of source documents need to be translated into, say, French, Italian, German and Spanish (often referred to as FIGS). The way you store your files will depend on the way you manage your files but a simple way of storing work records is in Microsoft Windows Explorer. The phases of production are

- The use of appropriate resources (you will have checked availability before acceptance of the work from the customer).
- Translation.
- Dealing with queries on terminology etc.
- Checking, proof reading and other pre-delivery checks.
- Possible revision of the basis of customer comments and changes.

A hypothetical directory hierarchy in Windows Explorer is shown in Figure 8.

The use of proprietary software will be adequate when starting your business but, as the level of departmentalisation becomes more complex, your may need to consider the

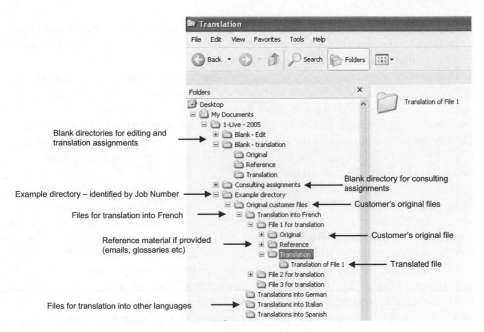

Figure 8. Example of a directory tree structure

need to introduce software that can integrate all the element of administration, production and accounting.

Production and quality control

The principal tasks of the production and quality control department are:

- The provision of internal translation production for the company's core languages.
- Quality control of outsourced translation assignments.
- Maintenance of reference material.
- Assisting in the assessment of enquiries from freelance enquiries and compiling a resources database in collaboration with the Administration Department.

Internal translation production

The scope of this department will be determined by the level of translation work done in-house and the amount of quality control done on the work of freelance translators. Organisations that provide translation services are structured in different ways and the perception held by buyers of translation services is diffuse. Most organisations are lumped under the term 'translation agencies'. This is all very well if the customer knows precisely what he is buying.

In general a translation agency acts as a broker by passing translation assignments to suitable freelances and charging the customer for providing a brokerage service. The agency may not have the skills or capacity to perform any translation quality control on the translation and is totally reliant on the integrity and skills of the translator. Depending on the purpose of the translation the agency may offer additional quality control by sending the translation to a second translator for checking and verification. A charge will be made for this service.

A translation company will have in-house translators and checkers for a specific range of languages but, in all probability, will also act as a broker of translation services that are not covered by in-house resources. As we have already mentioned, translation agencies and companies offer services in 'all languages' and 'all subjects'. As you can imagine, a comprehensive database of freelance service providers is needed to support this level of service.

Offer only the languages and subject areas that you know your organisation can provide while maintaining an acceptable level of quality. This is why it is important to test or verify the skills of applicants who wish to be included on your freelance database. You can add to the range of services you offer as your verified database increases in scope.

Quality control of outsourced translations

The level of and responsibility for quality control needs to be discussed and agreed clearly with the customer. Ultimately the company is responsible for the quality of the services provided to customers but it is unrealistic to expect to have in-house resources to check every translation that is supplied – what is the obligation of agencies that offer 'all subjects and all languages' in their advertising? Apart from competence in the language combinations provided in-house, there has to be total reliance on the skills of the freelance contracted for an assignment. Checking by a second person can be offered but the cost of this has to be factored into the agreed project cost.

Maintenance of reference material

What words of advice to a fledgling entrepreneur would I offer regarding reference material? Try and save any dictionaries and references that are relevant to your work – the Internet is not the be all and end all. I have, for example, a number of Swedish reference works that are no longer in print including a set of encyclopaedias and a Swedish/English maritime dictionary – both from the 1930s. These, and others, are invaluable when researching historical and cultural texts. Take the time and trouble to understand cultural differences. Nurture all the contacts you make and keep them alive.

Contacts can form the basis of most useful sources of reference material and I make no apology for repeating the advice about business cards. When somebody gives you their business card, don't just give it a cursory glance – take the time to read it (both front and back) and, without sounding or being patronising, ask a question or two before putting it in your briefcase or wallet for later filing. For this you will be remembered far more than somebody who just stuffs the card in his pocket without further ado.

It is inevitable that a large amount of reference material will be assembled in the form of dictionaries, specialist subject literature, customer reference material etc. A lot of this will be in printed format. There will also be the need to store material in electronic format and this will include terminology databases, translation memories and material researched on the internet.

It is important that this material be managed and stored in a manner that facilitates its retrieval.

Freelance resources database

The management of the freelance resources database can be done together the administration department since each freelance translator needs to be assessed for suitability.

Human resources

As the organisation grows there will be the need to consider what human resources will be needed. Most translation organisations rely considerably of freelances and this is a mutually-beneficial arrangement in most cases. There may come a time when it is more appropriate to have an employed member of staff to take on specific responsibilities. In my case, I ran a company whose principal market was Scandinavia and, for this purpose, we had several in-house translators and checkers working with Danish, Swedish and Norwegian.

The organisation and its industry

What are the intended activities of the organisation?

It is tempting to endeavour to be 'all things for all men' but it is best to offer only those services that you can offer through the resources you have and which you know you can develop. One of the beauties about the translation profession is the interdependence between translation agencies and freelance translators. This allows agencies to develop an extensive database of freelances and thereby meet the demands of a range of customers and industries.

Translation is still an unregulated profession and there are few restrictions on setting up a translation business. One restriction can be what you intend calling your organisation. Obviously you cannot use a name that is already registered nor can you use a business name that is misleading or inappropriate. Careful consideration should be given to this since it can have an impact on the credibility of your organisation when marketing your services.

Translation agency or translation company?

What's the difference? In the true sense of the word a translation agency acts purely as a broker of services whereas a translation company has its own in-house production resources.

In reality most serious providers of translation services fall somewhere in between the two inasmuch as they broker resources but also provide added value through project management, document engineering and additional quality control. For the sake of practicality I'll refer to both as translation agencies.

It is unrealistic for an agency to have resources for checking every translation that it handles particularly since translation is such a cost-led business. Thus the responsibility for translation quality control usually lies with the translator unless agreed otherwise even though the agency is responsible directly to its customers for the quality of the deliverables. The purpose for which the translation is made will determine the level of quality control. In extreme cases a back translation is made into the source language is to compare this with the original text but this is usually prohibitive in terms of time and cost. It would be better to ensure that an appropriate translator with the right skills is engaged from the outset.

Marketing the organisation's products and services

No organisation is purely a product organisation since every company's offerings contain a product element and a service element. Translation is a professional service but translators produce a tangible product in the form of a written translation.

Market forces and how you deal with them can determine whether your business will be successful or not. The list below identifies some of the issues you need to consider and these will evolve as the company evolves.

Corporate development

- Description of the organisation's products or services and their applications.
- What are the distinctive qualities of the products or services – these are often referred to as the company's USPs – unique selling points or KFSs – key factors for success.

- What technologies are required for the organisation's activities?
- What human resources are required for the organisation's activities?
- What skills are required for the organisation's activities?
- Does the organisation need to be concerned with licences or patent rights?
- What is the future potential for the organisation?
- Who will be the organisation's customers?
- Who will be the organisation's competitors?
- What market segments will the organisation be operating in?
- What is or what will be the organisation's market size and growth?
- What is or what will be the organisation's market share?
- What are the critical product or service characteristics or uniqueness?
- What is or what will be the response from your competitors?

One way to look at translation is as a system. The basic elements of this are illustrated in the following:

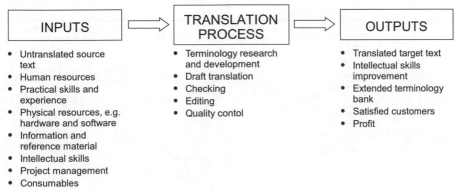

Figure 9.   Translation as a system

Added value

It is unlikely that your company will be successful unless your potential customer can readily identify the added value that you offer. Figure 10 below identifies elements of translation production that provide added value. Although translation tends to be a cost-led service, the provision of added value will be a greater selling point and justify more attractive rates. This is where your selling skills come into play. Rather that discussing price as the only criterion, try and determine how you can add value for which your customer will be prepared to pay. Primary activities are those which are more obvious to a customer whereas support activities are those which the customer is unaware of.

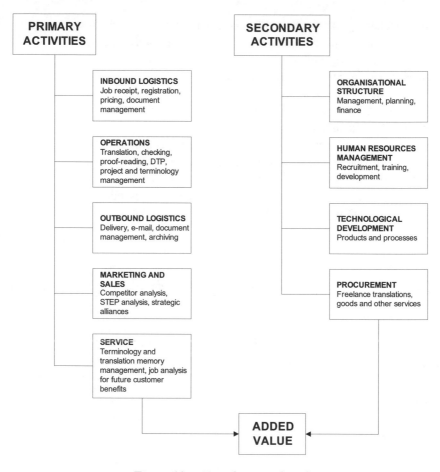

Figure 10 .   Translation value chain

When assessing your added value consider the following issues.

- How do your critical product or service characteristics compare to those of your competitors?
- What is your pricing policy?
- What is your selling policy?
- What is your distribution policy?
- How do you plan to advertise and promote your products or services?
- What is your policy for customer support?
- How do you plan to deal with complaints?

- What interest in shown in your products or services by potential customers?
- What added value do your products or service provide?

The following identifies the primary activities that may be obvious to a potential customer. Support activities are less obvious to the customer but nonetheless important to the quality of the final product.

Developing services

The phases in the life of a service of product can be described in four phases – conception, development, profitable phase and decline as illustrated in the following:

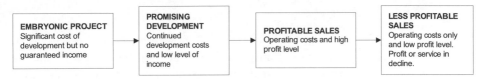

Figure 11. Product or service life

The embryonic phase can be based on an idea or objective that is unproven. A market analysis will determine whether the service is potentially viable. Probing questions need to be asked and the concept has to be carefully analysed before being launched. It has potential but costs money to develop without generating any income.

The growth phase shows more promise but continues to cost money. However it starts to generate income. Its rate of growth will determine whether or not the service is worth continuing. Compare growth against forecast and whether your return on investment is acceptable.

The next phase will hopefully be the profitable phase during which the service requires a minimum of resources to operate but generates income and a good profit. This is not the time to be complacent since there will always be competitors who will be attempting to do the same thing. There will also be the emergence of substitute products and low-cost services providers. This is the time to consider how you might develop new aspects of your business while you have the cash for investment. Each product or service has a finite life so don't wait too late before considering your options.

Finally there is the decline phase where a minimum of resources are required but where the services generate low profit. This can however be acceptable if you develop this service as a niche market. Delivering 'trade translations' is an example. If you have particular skills you may consider selling these to other translation companies albeit at a lower profit level.

4   An Introduction to Quality Management

My experience shows that trying to apply quality control to intellectual output such as translation is difficult and encounters significant resistance among practitioners. This is because translation is interpretation and therefore individual. As you may have experienced, style is the greatest bone of contention and the benchmark when dealing with a difference of opinion regarding style is 'Is the style of the translation and use of terminology appropriate for the intended purpose?' Quality management can however be more easily applied to the processes that support translation production.

GIGO is an acronym that many translators are familiar with and means Garbage In Garbage Out. In other words, if the source text is of poor quality there is a considerable risk that the quality of the resulting translation will be questionable. My own experience shows that this is often the case since a source text may have been written by somebody who is not articulate or does not have the source language as his mother tongue.

ISO 9001:2000

The international standard, quite often referred to as ISO 9001:2000, can provide a model for a quality management system without the organisation necessarily seeking accreditation to the standard. No serious organisation should be without a documented quality management system since this offers several advantages:

- It sets goals for the organisation to live up to.
- It can provide evidence to customers that the organisation takes quality seriously.
- It can provide a reference and training guide to new and existing employees.
- It considers issues such as customer focus and benchmarking that can support marketing and sales.

Be aware that this standard does not apply specifically to the quality of a particular translation – it applies more to the business processes that support project management.

Compiling a quality manual is a useful exercise in self-examination and, if you look at issues from your customer's perspective, it will give you a better idea of how you should structure your services.

Each organisation is unique in the skills it has and the service it offers but I hope the following will provide a useful guide on how to compile a quality management system for your own translation organisation. I run a limited company and I am the sole employee at present but what follows is easily adapted to a larger organisation. For the purpose of the quality manual I am referred to as the managing director since this is my formal position in the company according to its memorandum and articles of association. When you compile your quality manual you will need to identify the person who is responsible for implementation of the relevant parts of the quality manual.

How you compile your quality management system is a personal choice but if you work to a recognised standard and wish to seek accreditation you can use ISO 9004:2000, Quality Management systems – Guidelines for performance improvements, as a model. This chapter is based on the quality management system I have compiled for my own business that covers the skills that I am qualified to offer – freelance translation, lecturing and business consultancy. It is also based on my experience of managing a translation company with 15 employees – the company was accredited to ISO 9002:1994 which has now been superseded by ISO 2001:2000.

Formal accreditation requires internal audits to be conducted twice a year by the organisation's quality representative as well as a surveillance visit made once a year by an assessor from the accreditation body that awarded accreditation to ISO 9001:2000.

It may appear strange to have a quality management system for a 'one-man-band' but consider this from a marketing aspect as well as the benefits that a formal system offers:

- You have a competitive advantage since you can demonstrate to potential customers that you take quality seriously and have compiled procedures, instructions and other documentation to facilitate quality control.
- Your organisation could be excluded from bidding for certain work if you do not have a formal quality management system.
- If a customer voices a complaint, you will already have considered how you might deal with such an issue. Obviously nobody likes receiving complaints but if you resolve a complaint in a factual, objective and impartial way your customer will see that you have taken the complaint seriously.

Having to deal with a customer complaint is time-consuming and never a pleasant task. It is necessary to accept that a customer complaint could arise even though the complaint is unfounded. A detailed flowchart showing the procedure for resolving a customer complaint is given in Appendix 6.

Just for the record, I carried out 115 assignments in 2004. One customer complaint was received which, after investigation, was considered unwarranted by the agency who commissioned the translation and which resulted in no further action by end customer. The report submitted subsequent to investigation is also shown after the detailed flowchart referred to above.

European standard for translation services

At long last there is the emergence of a European standard for translation services. I welcome this wholeheartedly because it will set a benchmark for the profession and a recognised level of quality management for translation service providers. Among the issues covered by the standard are:

- Human resources management.
- Professional competencies of translators, revisers and reviewers.
- Continuing professional development.
- Quality management.
- Client – Translation Service Provider management.
- Procedures in translation services.
- Added value services.

In my experience going back to attempts to introduce BS5750 as a benchmark in the Translators Guild (from which the embryonic ITI evolved) there has always been resistance from some translators who have questioned the right of any reader of their translation to offer criticism. I always welcome criticism since, if it is valid and constructive, it can add to your knowledge. If it is not valid you can disregard it while confirming that your translation is correct.

The standard offers both translation service providers and their clients a transparent description and definition of the entire process. At the same time the standard is designed to provide translation service providers with a set of procedures and standard requirements to enable them to meet market requirements. Certification is envisaged for translation service providers who satisfy the requirements of this standard.

There are people who bemoan the fact that translation is not recognised as a serious profession and does not attract the remuneration and rewards it deserves. Surely working to a recognised and documented standard and gaining certification according to the standard set can only enhance the standing of the profession?

I accept that qualification for membership of a professional organisation such as the Institute of Linguists or the Institute of Translation and Interpreting sets specific benchmarks but these are probably viewed as internal issues by an uninformed public. I feel that certification by an independent body such as the European Committee for Standardization, and which CEN member countries are bound to comply with, should be encouraged and implemented by all translation service providers who aspire to gaining public recognition and abolishing the stereotypical view held of translators.

Notwithstanding this I recognise that anybody can still call themselves a translator and practice as such and, while the profession remains largely unregulated, this will remain the case.

Documented quality management from the outset

Most organisations start from an idea or goal of an individual person and develop from there. Looking at quality as a serious issue from the start sets the tone and allows your organisation to grow in a structured manner.

Depending on the resources available I would suggest that it takes about a year to have a fully-working, documented and accredited quality management system. The process is shown in the following and identifies the different stages that need to be considered. Compiling such a quality system is an iterative process since procedures and instructions need to be put into practice and modified on the basis of implementation and experience. Realistically, it takes several months to get to a stage where compliance can be assessed. Documentation needs to be assessed first and implemented for a reasonable time to gather evidence that the system is realistic, relevant and appropriate.

Glossary of terms used in quality management

Contract	Documentation of terms agreed with a customer covering the scope of the work to be done.
Instruction	Defines and explains how a task is to be performed.
Job bag	The term used to describe a plastic folder, cardboard folder or ring binder containing all the information and documentation related to a project whether this be in electronic or hard-copy format.
Non-compliance	The non-fulfilment or non-adherence to laid-down specifications or regulations.

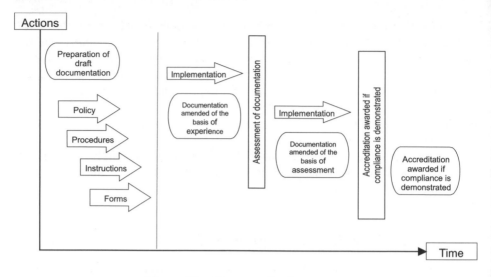

Figure 12.   The accreditation process

Non-conformity	The failure to meet specified quality requirements for a product or service, the assessment of which does not depend on the passage of time.
Procedure	Defines how tasks or operations are to be managed.
Product	A generic term used to describe the either the product or service that the company delivers. It can be argued that there is no pure service and no pure product since each contains an element of the other.
Project	A generic term used to define the scope of the work carried out for a customer such as translation, providing business advice and producing reports.
Project documentation	This includes all documentation generated as an intrinsic part of a project and includes translations, reports and presentations.
Quality	Fitness for purpose or meeting customer requirements.
Quality assurance	Planned and systematic actions necessary to provide adequate confidence that a product or service will satisfy given requirements.
Quality audit	A systematic and independent examination to determine whether quality activities and related results comply with planned arrangements and whether these arrangements are implemented effectively and are suitable for achieving objectives.

Quality management	That aspect of the overall management function that determines and implements the quality policy.
Quality policy	The overall quality intentions and direction of the organisation in relation to quality as formally expressed by the management.
Quality system	The organisational structure, responsibilities, procedures, processes and resources for implementing quality management.

Figure 12 shows that an accredited quality management system comprises four main parts:

1. Quality policy.
2. Quality procedures.
3. Work instructions.
4. Forms and supporting documentation.

The following sections look at these in detail.

Quality policy

In addition to determining what your quality policy shall cover it can also be used for marketing purposes. It is likely that you will be asked what your quality policy is so rather than making a bland statement you will be able to provide your potential customer with tangible evidence of your concern for quality.

The following provides a model which can be used to formulate a policy that is appropriate for your own organisation. How you formulate this depends on the scope of your business but the following can provide a starting point.

XYZ Translation Services Ltd. is a privately-owned company dedicated to the provision of high quality services to its customers. These services comprise:

- Translation of documentation between (*range of languages*) in the following areas (*list subject areas*)
- Related services that include (*list services that might include checking, proof-reading and editing, other elements of quality control, document engineering and localisation*).

Translation

This is where you can state the resources you have to meet customer requirements. This might be articulated as follows:

> The company has its own staff translators, project managers and support staff plus an extensive database of freelance translators that have been assessed and tested (consider how you might do this) to ensure they have the appropriate skills and experience for this purpose.

Company organisation

Depending on the size and structure of your organisation you can show this as an organisation chart and identify who is responsible for different quality procedures and aspects of quality management.

You need to state who is responsible for the various activities carried out by the company. Small, embryonic businesses used to have a hard time getting established since many potential customers preferred to do business with substantial and established service providers. Small businesses (micro-companies sounds better!) can react to change and demands perhaps more quickly than large businesses. This is particularly the case where a significant amount of the company's resources are provided through sub-contractors and freelances.

Quality responsibilities

Quality responsibilities cover the following activities:

a)   Issuing and maintaining the company's quality documentation including the Quality Policy, the Procedures and any other documents necessary to control the quality of the company's operations.
b)   Planning and implementing the company's quality audit system.
c)   Performing regular reviews of the company's performance.
d)   Analysing customer complaint forms.
e)   Determining and implementing actions to correct recurrent discrepancies arising from the analyses carried out under d) above.

Commercial responsibilities

Commercial responsibilities cover the following activities:

a)   The efficient operation of all contracts undertaken by the company.
b)   Financial aspects of the company's business including accounts.
c)   Maintaining the existing customer base and seeking new customers.
d)   Analysing the totality of enquiries received and considering any changes in policy that could be beneficial to the company in operating cost-effectively.

e)   The receipt and safe storage, and return if required, of material supplied by the customers. This seldom arises when dealing with documents in electronic format but a customer might lend you an example of a product for which you are producing translations. You may be asked to provide certified translations of original documents so the issue of safe storage can be very important.

Purpose

The purpose of a quality policy is to ensure that it provides a means for leading the company towards improvement of its performance. Annual customer satisfaction surveys, recording *ad hoc* customer comments and appropriate action, and processing customer complaints are used as a basis for structuring continuous improvement. These will determine:

- The level and type of future improvement needed for the organisation.
- The expected or desired degree of customer satisfaction.

Such measures will be augmented by maintaining a watching brief to ensure that customer satisfaction is maintained through:

- Compiling simple statistics to record timeliness of delivery and action taken in the event of customer complaints.
- Assessment and continuous personal development of person(s) used to provide the service offered by the company.
- The application of resources in addition to ISO 9001:2000 requirements such as certification of translations.
- The potential contribution of sub-contractors.

Commitment

This is based on the assumption that you will work according to a documented quality management system. It does not necessarily mean that you have to seek accreditation although this does offer a degree of competitive advantage.

This can be confirmed by demonstrating that the company has introduced systems and procedures which ensure that work performed is governed by the requirements laid down in ISO 9001:2000. By this means, the company ensures that the requirements of its customers are established at the earliest practicable time, that these requirements are followed, and that the achievement of the requirements is closely monitored.

Records must be kept of all the important activities undertaken by the company. These records are analysed periodically as part of a systematic audit both to highlight and to correct any areas of weakness within the company and to seek out means of further improving the company's performance.

This Quality Policy document, and the procedures to which it refers, contains the details of the company's approach to meeting these aims. Where necessary, the procedures are augmented by instructions that are prepared to ensure that each aspect of the work is performed in a consistent manner.

All the company documents referred to above are periodically reviewed to ensure their continuing effectiveness in meeting the company's aims.

Quality gap analysis

There is the potential for quality gaps to arise unless there is clear, unambiguous specification of what needs to be done from when a customer decides to commission a translation to when that translation is delivered. This is considered in the following quality gap analysis.

Quality gap	How the quality gap arises
Gap 1 – the gap between what the customer expects and the project manager's understanding of what the customer wants	The gap arises when the project manager does not understand what the customer considers to be important to the translation process. The customer may expect a perfectly-formatted, independently-checked and edited translation (although has not specifically stated so) whereas the project manager believes that the translation will be used for information purposes only and requires no special layout.
Gap 2 – the gap between the project manager's perception of what the customer wants and the actual specification for the translation	The gap arises when the project manager does not draw up a specification that is detailed enough to show clearly what is required. This may leave the translator who actually carries out the translation unsure about what exactly is intended. The gap may be a consequence of the translation requirements not being stated adequately by the customer. For example, the customer may expect the translation to be provided in a particular software format whereas the translator is not informed of this.
Gap 3 – the gap between the customer specification and how the customer views what is delivered	This gap arises when the delivered translation does not correspond to what was specified by the customer. One example is the translation being longer than expected. It is the customer's perception that is important but there may be a number of intangible factors that were not anticipated.
Gap 4 – the gap between the customer's experience and external communication to the customer.	This arises when the translation provider cannot deliver what is promised in advertising or promotion material. In other words, the translation provider must make sure that what is promised is, in fact, delivered.

Quality gap	How the quality gap arises
Gap 5 – the gap between the customer's expectation and the customer's experience	A customer's expectation is affected by his own experiences, the recommendations of others and the claims made by the translation services provider. The translation services provider must bear in mind that the customer's experience is determined by his perception of what is supplied, not by the perception held by the translation services provider.

Table 3. Quality gaps that can arise in translation

The principal quality objectives in translation are:

- To understand the customer requirements so that no quality gaps arise and the customer requirements are met.
- To provide the resources to meet the requirements of the work.

More specific quality objectives are determined by the intended use for the translation and can be defined as follows:

- To provide the appropriate linguistic skills and experience.[3]
- To provide an accurate and complete translation.
- To deliver on or before the agreed delivery date and time.
- To deliver work in the software prescribed by the customer.
- To use terminology appropriate for the intended use.

The quality of the translation's content and layout are often better than that of the source document. This is particularly the case if the original text author is inexperienced in the use of text templates and style sheets. The layout may be prescribed by the customer of course.

Unless stated otherwise by the customer the usual assumption is that translation is for information only. It is better to ask rather than assume since, in all probability, the customer may be unaware of what goes on in the translation process. Specific quality requirements noted by the customer will be recorded on the work order form.

Project management services

Project management services can cover arrange of issues associated with the services that the company offers and can include working at a customer's premises.

---

3. A requirement can be that translator should be a Member of the Institute of Translation and Interpreting (or equivalent body), should have a working knowledge of the subject being translated and at least three years' full-time experience.

Project quality objectives are determined by the scope of the project and are defined as follows:

- To provide the appropriate project management skills and experience required for the project.
- To produce and manage the relevant project documentation.
- To ensure that the work covered by the project is delivered on or before the agreed delivery date and time.
- To deliver work in the format prescribed by the customer.
- To adhere to style and layout prescribed by the customer.
- To use terminology appropriate for the intended use.

Benchmarking and quality management

The nature of the translation profession and the type of services provided need careful consideration to determine useful and practical benchmarks against which to assess output and customer satisfaction. This is often a challenge since there is sometimes no direct contact with the end customer when working for other translation agencies or other intermediaries.

Benchmarking the company

The company's translation services are principally intellectual output and the scope for benchmarking is often limited by factors beyond the company's control. These include:

- The quality of the source text to be translated – the author may not be a native speaker of the source text. This can present its own unique challenges.
- The inability to talk directly to the source text author.
- reluctance by the customer to accept constructive criticism on the source text.
- Who or what determines the quality of the output.

Tangible benchmarks against which services can be measured are:

- The number of customer complaints per 100 assignments – justified and unjustified.
- The percentage of deliveries made before or on time.
- The volume or repeat business from a customer.

Project management services can be benchmarked in the same manner and, although the output is still essentially intellectual, there is often more direct contact with the customer. There are also tangible project objectives that can be benchmarked.

Benchmarking customers

The principal benchmarks that can be applied to customers are:

- The level of information provided and its impact on the company's production.
  - provision of an order confirmation that includes a purchase order number and delivery date that has been agreed.
  - name of a project manager or contact person to whom queries can be addressed.

- The quality of the source material and its impact on the time spent on the project.
  - how much time is spent preparing a text for translation – this is particularly relevant when using translation memory software.
  - how much time is spent resolving queries on the text with the customer.
  - how much time is spent researching terminology etc.

- Payment discipline by customer and its impact on the company's financial performance.
  - compiling a record of invoice dates.
  - dates when payments are due.
  - dates when payments were made.
  - debtor days per customer to identify slow payers.
  - average debtor days.

A record of payment discipline can be compiled using an Excel spreadsheet, for example. Invoices are issued on completion of work with a reminder sent at the end of the payment period if payment is not made. Remember that the cost of chasing unpaid invoices and the time taken amounts to a loss of resources that can be devoted to other work.

Experience and records will show which customers need reminding to provide the necessary information. Always keep copies of relevant emails and other correspondence so that these can be referred to in the event of any dispute.

Benchmarking that is specific to customer relations is dealt with in Chapter 8.

Quality framework

Quality systems

The procedures which are operated by the company to comply with the policy statement in the Quality Manual are contained in the Operating Procedures section of the Quality

Manual. Where necessary, Work Instructions, which detail the specific tasks to be carried out, are provided to augment these procedures.

The effective implementation of these procedures is monitored by planned audits and other monitoring and reporting techniques, all of which are detailed in the Operating Procedures Manual. The results of all such monitoring activities are reviewed by the Managing Director (or the Quality Manager who has the delegated responsibility) at the regular Management Review meetings. A result of these meetings is the planning of actions to improve the operation of the company either as a result of discrepancies found or suggestions put forward. The method of monitoring the effectiveness of the actions forms part of this planning process.

Where it is recognised that additional techniques, resources and skills are required to meet the requirements of a specific contract or a general future customer requirement, the acquisition of these is carried out in a planned and controlled manner in order to ensure that the customers' needs are met in a timely manner.

Contract review

All enquiries received by the company are examined to ensure that they are clear and concise and fall within the scope of operation of the company. Where this is not so, or where the enquiry would lead to a significant increase of the manpower and equipment resources held by the company, the Quality Manager will make a decision on whether or not to tender for the work.

Where a quotation or estimate is accepted by the customer, the requirements of the order placed are checked against the quotation to ensure that there are no significant differences.

If an amendment is made to a contract where a Work Order Form has been raised, but before work on that contract has been commenced, a new offer (quotation) is submitted to the customer for approval. A new contract is made when the customer accepts the revised offer and a revised Work Order Form is raised.

If an amendment is proposed while work is in progress, agreement on the scope and cost of the amended contract is to be agreed with the customer and noted on an amended Work Order Form. An amendment may be noted on the original Work Order Form if the change is minor.

Document and data control

All documents produced by the company which may have an affect on the quality of the service provided, including this quality policy, the operating procedures and the work instructions, are subject to controls which ensure that:

a)   They are authorised, prior to their issue, by the Quality Manager.

b)   They are issued in a controlled manner which ensures that they are available where they are needed and at the time when they are needed.
c)   Any changes made are authorised by the Quality Manager.
d)   The nature and extent of the change is, wherever practicable, indicated on the reissued document.
e)   The up-issued documents are filed in the quality control manual and the obsolete copies removed and destroyed.

Control of internal documents

According to the quality standard ISO 9004:2000, documents required by the quality management system shall be controlled. Controlled documents are those that are current and issued on a controlled basis to identified members of staff. All documents are stored in electronic format. The electronic files are the definitive versions of the documents and all controlled copies need to be identified as such. A list must be kept to show who has received controlled copies. All other copies of quality manual documents constitute uncontrolled copies.

Controlled documents come under three categories – active, review and obsolete. The status of these is illustrated in Figure 13.

Internal documents are reviewed on a continuous basis and are amended when appropriate to reflect experience and improvements. All documents are issued in a controlled manner and require the approval of the Quality Manager before being issued.

Identification of project documentation

The means by which the identity of project documentation is maintained throughout the production process is contained within the operating procedures. The method of identification, through the use of a unique job number for each individual project that is noted in the Job Book, enables traceability to be undertaken should this ever become a requirement.

How you identify project documentation is a matter of personal choice but should permit ease of identification and traceability. Project documentation is identified by either a unique alphanumeric job name or a customer's job name if so required by that customer. An example of a document tree that identifies documents is given in Figure 8.

There may be a need to trace documents. Why?

- A customer may require the later revision or update of a document already translated. Being able to look at the previous assignment particularly for terminology is essential. The diligent use of translation memory software and terminology management will of course facilitate this task.

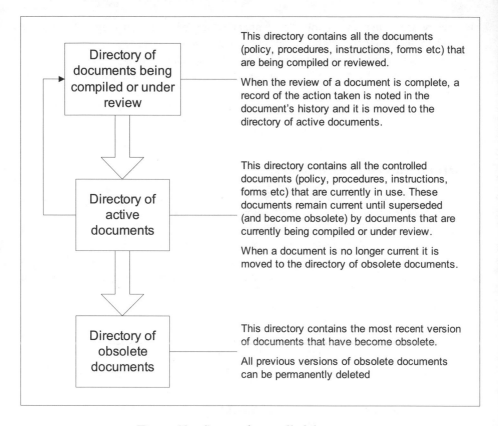

Figure 13.   Status of controlled documents

- There may be printed copies of reference material related to a past job that is not stored in electronic format.
- A customer complaint could conceivably arise some time after the translation was delivered. Tracing documents related to the assignment then becomes necessary.

Control of external documents

The control of identified documents of external origin shall be maintained through consultation with the issuer of such documents prior to use to ensure that such documents are valid. XYZ Translation Services Ltd is kept advised on quality issues and amendments to quality documents such as ISO 9001:2000 through the service it receives from its assessment body.

External documents such as British Standards purchased for a particular assignment or project are expected to be current at the date of purchase and will be identified as such.

Data control

Data held in databases and terminology banks on the company's computers shall be controlled and maintained. All such data should be password-protected where appropriate to prevent unauthorised use and to preclude the use of invalid and/or obsolete documents.

Electronic copies of project documentation are archived in the ARCHIVE directory under the respective customer's sub-directory and job folder.

Electronic files can be backed up on a separate rewriteable CD. There can be a separate CD for each working day, i.e. Monday to Friday. A weekly backup can also be also made and stored off site. The manner in which this is done will be determined by the scope of the company's operations. Day-to-day work can be temporarily stored on what is referred to a memory stick whose capacity is usually more than adequate for storing a day's production.

Purchasing

Orders placed for products or services to support the undertaking of the products or services offered by the company are directed to vendors who have a reputation for the quality of their products within their industry or profession.

All purchase orders are checked to ensure that they clearly state requirements and authorised prior to their release for purchase.

It is seldom that there will be a requirement to allow customers access to the premises of vendors or other suppliers for verification or other monitoring purposes since the company does not perform work for customers at such premises. This is particularly the case where the company uses freelances since the company itself will be directly responsible for their output.

Project management

All contracts entered into by the company are planned to ensure that the skills and resources necessary to meet the requirements of the contract are available. Where necessary this planning will include selecting suitable staff to undertake each activity required to fulfil the contract, ensuring that reference material is available where this is appropriate, defining the standard to which the work is to be carried out, and the format and means of delivery.

Process activities are carried out, controlled and monitored as per procedures and customer requirements. The general process of translation is illustrated in Figure 6.

Pre-delivery checks on translations

Translations and other related tasks are checked, as required by written procedures, for conformance with the requirements at various stages during the translation process or editing process. These checks, the level of which is determined by the end usage to which the translation is to be put, are carried out on completion of the translation or other work ordered by the customer.

Where, for whatever reason, translations are released from the company without the completion of any or all of the checking or correctional activities, steps are taken to ensure that the customer is in agreement with this action. This may arise if the translation assignment is cancelled before it is completed. The necessary checking activities are undertaken after delivery and the translation replaced where significant errors are discovered.

A Work Order Form contains a list of pre-delivery checks. These pre-delivery checks are to be performed before the work is dispatched to the customer and the electronic copy of the completed work is transferred to the ARCHIVE directory on the computer. Checks are confirmed by entering a tick in the appropriate boxes. The relevant part of the Work Order Form for translation assignments is shown below. This assumes that all written documents are stored for a minimum of three years.

The scope of these pre-delivery checks may be such that they cannot be accommodated on a simple Work Order Form. The project manager will agree these with the customer and they can be recorded on a separate project sheet. Reference to this must be made on the Work Order Form if a separate sheet is used.

Project status

The status of a translation is indicated by a means which enables the conformance or otherwise of each translation to be readily established at any time during the translation or project report-writing process including any advanced release authorised by the customer.

Work in progress recorded on computer is located in the LIVE directory in a sub-directory identified by the job number or the customer's designation. When all the pre-delivery checks have been carried out, the translation project is signed off and transferred to the ARCHIVE directory and stored in a sub-directory identified by the customer's name and the job number/customer job name.

The same applies to project reports once they have been approved by the customer.

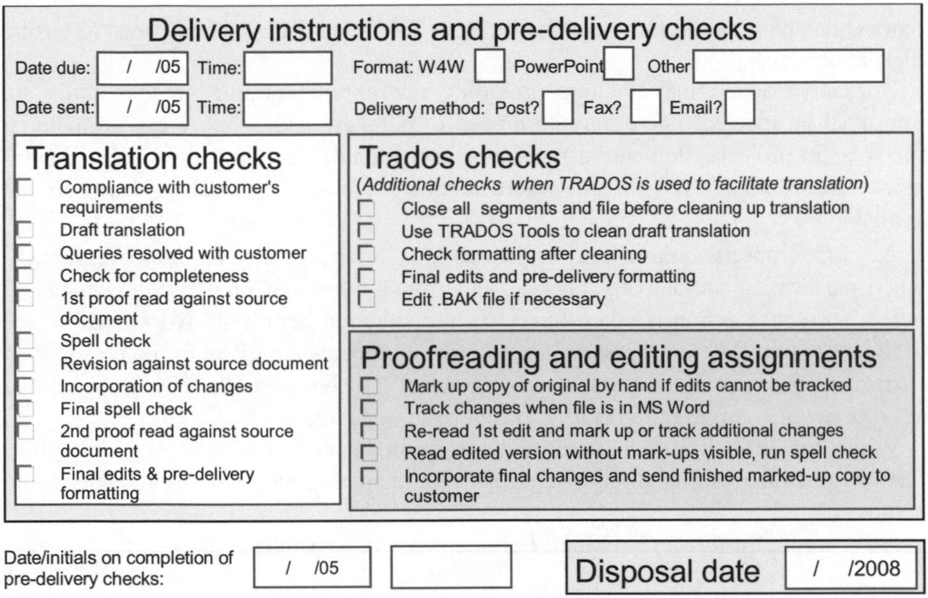

Delivery instructions and pre-delivery checks

Date due: __ /05 Time: ____   Format: W4W ☐ PowerPoint ☐ Other ____

Date sent: __ /05 Time: ____   Delivery method: Post? ☐ Fax? ☐ Email? ☐

Translation checks

☐ Compliance with customer's requirements
☐ Draft translation
☐ Queries resolved with customer
☐ Check for completeness
☐ 1st proof read against source document
☐ Spell check
☐ Revision against source document
☐ Incorporation of changes
☐ Final spell check
☐ 2nd proof read against source document
☐ Final edits & pre-delivery formatting

Trados checks

(Additional checks when TRADOS is used to facilitate translation)

☐ Close all segments and file before cleaning up translation
☐ Use TRADOS Tools to clean draft translation
☐ Check formatting after cleaning
☐ Final edits and pre-delivery formatting
☐ Edit .BAK file if necessary

Proofreading and editing assignments

☐ Mark up copy of original by hand if edits cannot be tracked
☐ Track changes when file is in MS Word
☐ Re-read 1st edit and mark up or track additional changes
☐ Read edited version without mark-ups visible, run spell check
☐ Incorporate final changes and send finished marked-up copy to customer

Date/initials on completion of pre-delivery checks: __ /05 ____

Disposal date __ /2008

Figure 14. Delivery instructions and pre-delivery checks

Control of non-conforming translations

Non-conforming translations are those that do not meet the required standards and are identified in a manner which indicates that they are unsuitable for delivery to the customer.

The level of quality control performed by a supplier of translation services (i.e. agency) varies and it is often not possible, practical or cost-effective to have every translation independently checked or assessed. This is why it is so important to have the competence of the translator assessed. The level of quality control possible must be agreed before an assignment is accepted.

Any problems identified by end users or customers are processed as customer complaints.

Where the customer authorises the delivery of the non-conforming translation, a record of this authorisation is attached to the translation.

Corrective and preventive action

Complaints from customers and other sources are investigated to establish the cause(s) and, where appropriate, actions are planned and implemented to prevent further occurrences. The planning of these actions includes the monitoring of the actions to ensure their effectiveness.

Corrective action may include providing appropriate training so that skills are improved or updated. There may be a need to purchase additional reference material for specific projects. Preventive measures may include declining translation assignments or consultancy assignments where adequate reference material and skills are not available.

Any error, observation or non-conformance is an opportunity for improvement. If, when performing pre-delivery checks, an error, observation or non-conformance is noted, corrective action is taken to rectify the situation before the work is delivered to the customer. Where necessary, constructive comments are given to the person who performed the work so that note can be taken of the comments thereby ensuring that appropriate preventive action is to prevent errors being repeated.

While it is difficult in some cases to be aware in advance of what errors might arise, forward planning can heighten awareness by anticipating where improvements could be possible.

An example Customer Complaint Form is given in Appendix 5.

Handling and storage

All documents and other media relevant to a project must be handled, stored, packaged and despatched in such a manner as to prevent their deterioration and/or damage.

All customer-supplied material, including the source document and reference material must be checked for adequacy and, once accepted, handled, stored and preserved in such a manner as to prevent loss or damage prior to its return to the customer.

Records

Records of quality activities are maintained in accordance with procedures which detail how these records are identified, collected, stored and maintained. The requirement to keep such records is given in the Quality Procedures Manual.

Communication and understanding

In a small business the quality organisation will probably be headed by one person who has prepared this policy and its associated documentation and will include those who implement it. In a larger organisation a designated person may have overall responsibility for this function as the quality manager. Any external person who performs an audit or survey is assumed to have sufficient knowledge of ISO 9001:2000 to understand the documentation on the quality management system.

An internal Quality Audit plan is drawn up by the Quality Manager on an annual basis in consultation with an independent auditor. This plan covers all the activities of the company which impact upon the quality of the service provided. The frequency of the audit of each area of operation is determined by the importance of the activity and the number of staff engaged upon it.

The results of these and the agreed recovery actions are reported to the Managing Director who monitors the implementation of the recovery actions at the Management Review meetings. The company's principal objective is to provide added value to the customer and to identify opportunities for continual improvement.

The Quality Policy is reviewed as a matter of course during periodic audits to ensure its relevance. Amendments may also be made when justified by commercial considerations. This is illustrated in Figure 15.

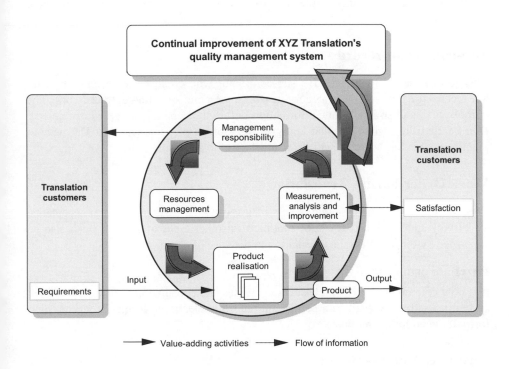

Figure 15. Continuous improvement of an organisation's quality management system

Forms used in quality management

Bureaucracy is intended to facilitate the work of the organisation and time should not be spent designing forms unless they have a specific purpose. Apply what is referred to as the So what? – test. If you can respond to the test with 'Which means that . . . ' and the information is useful then include the relevant part of the form. Modern technology means that forms and company stationery can be printed on demand and readily updated without the need to discard stocks of obsolescent versions.

As a company grows it may be appropriate to have an integrated data management system so that information does not need to be duplicated on different forms and during different stages of production from order to invoice. To try and describe such a system within the scope of this book would be unrealistic since its scope would determine how the system would be designed. As a consequence examples of a number of forms are provided in a format that can be readily copied and adapted for individual purposes. The maxim should be 'keep it simple'.

The forms included in this chapter are discussed below and examples are given in the Appendices.

Sub-contractor record

This form is sent to a prospective sub-contractor who could be a freelance translator, technical editor or other category to whom the company sub-contracts work. The purpose is to gather appropriate information before the person is accepted or rejected. Don't forget the regulations that apply to the storage of personal data. The general practice now is for this to be sent as an attachment to an email.

Work Order Form – Translation

This form identifies the essential details of a translation assignment from acceptance to delivery and invoicing. It can be modified for other types of service. I can also be supported by other project documentation in the case of complex projects.

Purchase order form

It is now common to make purchases for services and consumables on-line. Whatever system is used, there shall be a permanent record in electronic format or written on a form designed for the purpose.

Customer Complaint Form

This form identifies the various stages of dealing with a customer complaint. Importantly it records action to prevent recurrence irrespective of whether the complaint was justified or not.

Audit Plan

This records what is being audited during an internal audit on the date set aside for that audit. Different people who are responsible for specific procedures in the quality system will be audited accordingly.

Audit Report

The audit report summarises the results of the internal audit plus details of discrepancies (the non-compliances and observations raised).

Audit Discrepancy Report

The report identifies the quality discrepancy and what action is taken to rectify the same.

Job Application Form

A job application form is used to gather relevant information on any applicant for a job and to ask for consent to approach references that are given. It may be appropriate to seek professional advice to ensure that the form does not breach any legislation or code of practice. Make sure that the form is constructed so that it solicits useful and relevant information.

Job Interview Record

A job interview should include open questions that result in useful information that will be appropriate for the selection of the best candidate for a specific job. A question that elicits only a Yes or No response does not encourage an interviewee to respond with factual information or provides opinion that is helpful. Any candidate called for an interview should be sent a job description in good time before an interview.

An interview should be supplemented with a practical test where this is appropriate for the position. It is a fact of life that some people perform well at interviews but are not able to meet expectations in practice.

Encourage the interviewee to consider the interview a two-way process and thereby take the opportunity to 'interview' the company as a potential employer.

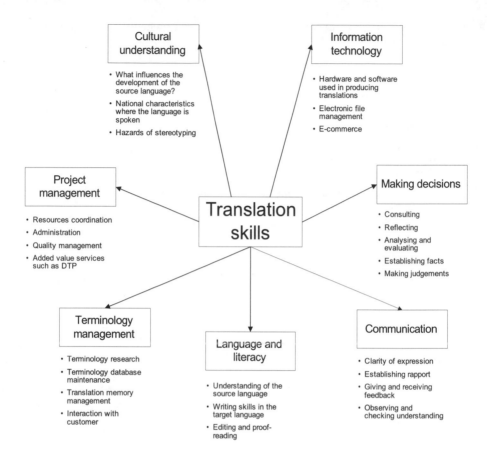

Figure 16.   Translation skills clusters

Non-disclosure agreement

As a knowledge organisation one of your most important assets is information. This covers a number of areas of which the following are but a few:

- Knowledge about your customer base.
- Knowledge about your business and the way it operates.
- Market intelligence.
- Your freelance translator database.
- Your pricing structure.
- Knowledge about your customer's business.

It is inevitable that some of this may be disclosed during an interview or when engaging sub-contractors. It is also likely that some of the knowledge about your customers will be confidential. This is why it is necessary to have a non-disclosure agreement. When formulating a non-disclosure agreement ensure that it can be enforceable if necessary.

Education and training record

The list of skills required for a staff translator, for example, are included in Figure 16.

Some of these will be included in the knowledge and skills that your staff bring with them when they join the organisation or gain as part of their continuous personal development. It is useful when compiling a job description to list the particular skills that are required for a specific job. During an interview this list can indicate what training may be necessary for the person to perform effectively and efficiently.

5   Quality Procedures

Procedures state what the company does to comply with the requirements of the quality management system. In some cases these are supplemented with work instructions that facilitate the understanding and implementation of procedures.

The responsibility for the implementation of quality procedures is that of the Managing Director or the Quality Manager with the delegated responsibility. This will probably be the same person in a small organisation. The name of the person responsible for a particular procedure shall be identified in that procedure.

The following give an indication of the procedures that are required for quality management in a translation company

Document control

Documents issued as part of a quality management system shall be controlled in an identifiable manner so that only the latest version of a procedure, instruction or form, etc. is used.

The purpose of this procedure is to lay down the responsibilities for the approval, issue and control of those documents used within the company that impact upon the quality of the company's products. This applies to the following:

- Quality documents contained in the Quality Manual.
- Forms associated with procedures and instructions contained in the Quality Manual.
- Output documents that are produced in the form of translations and project reports.
- An illustration of the controlled documents used in this procedure are given in Figure 18.

Control of documents

The master copy of the Quality Manual and its electronic version are stored on the computer in sub-directory C: . . . \ISO9001 2000\ACTIVE\. The Quality Manual includes the company's Quality Policy, quality procedures, instructions, and related forms. The Quality Manual, procedures and instructions are approved by the Quality Manager. All amendments to it are compiled by and require the approval of the Quality Manager.

Controlled procedures and documents bear the legend

'CONTROLLED DOCUMENT ONLY IF PRINTED IN COLOUR'

at the top of each page. All other copies in existence are uncontrolled copies. The quality policy, procedures and work instructions are controlled documents as illustrated in this procedure (see Figure 17).

Approval prior to issue

Documents used by the company and that have an impact on quality are designed to:

- Meet the requirements of the relevant section of ISO 9001:2000.
- Be appropriate for the intended purpose.
- Be consistent and written to facilitate comprehension, unambiguous interpretation and application.

Documents are then approved for issue by the Quality Manager.

Depending on their status, controlled documents are stored electronically in different directories as shown in the following structure for the first issue of this procedure, for example XYZ OPS 01 Issue A.

Document status

Active documents

Active documents are current issues in use and which are available in printed format in the company's quality manual and distributed to individuals as noted in the Distribution List in the Contents section of the company's Quality Manual. Active documents remain current until superseded by revised versions that have been approved by the Quality Manager. The most recent version of any document that is no longer valid is transferred to the relevant section of the Obsolete Documents directory.

Documents under review

Draft copies of all quality documents under review or being updated and which form part of the Quality Manual are controlled by the Quality Manager. They are stored in

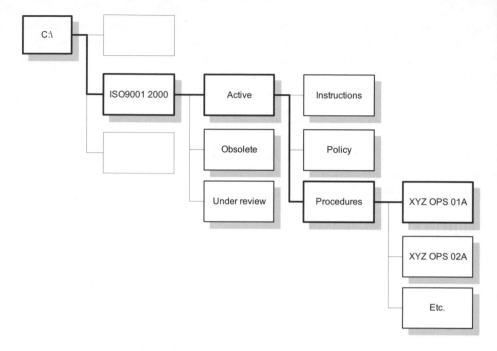

Figure 17.   Electronic storage of controlled documents

electronic format in the Under Review directory. The header of any review copy shall include the following legend.

'UNDER REVIEW'

Changes and the current revision status of controlled documents are identified by the document history on the front page and an issue letter in the header of each page. The latest issue of uncontrolled documents such as forms is identified in the Contents section of the company's Quality Manual.

Obsolete documents

The most recent version of any obsolete quality document is stored in electronic format in the Obsolete Documents directory. The header of any obsolete version shall include the following legend printed in red.

'OBSOLETE'

External documents

The control of identified documents of external origin shall be maintained through consultation with the issuer of such documents prior to use to ensure that such documents are valid. XYZ Translation Services is kept advised on quality issues and amendments to quality documents such as ISO 9001:2000 through the service it receives from its assessment body.

External documents such as British Standards purchased for a particular assignment or project are expected to be current at the date of purchase and will be identified as such.

Other documents

Register of forms

The masters of all the forms referred to in the Quality Procedures are contained in the Forms section of the quality manual.

Changes to the forms are made by the Quality Manager and the index to the register updated to reflect this. No stocks of forms are held since forms are printed out on demand. Obsolete versions of forms in electronic format are deleted from the computer. The latest versions of the forms are indicated by an issue letter and are identified in the list of forms at the beginning of the Forms section.

Production documents

Production documents, e.g. translations and project reports, are considered to be work in progress while stored in the LIVE directory on the computer. Electronic copies of completed translations and project reports are archived in the ARCHIVE directory under the respective customer's sub-directory and job folder.

Records

The previous issue of superseded parts of the Quality Manual, procedures and instructions is maintained by the Quality Manager. Previous issues are kept only in electronic format.

Where practical, hard copy versions of production documents are archived. Hardcopy documents are kept for a maximum of three years when they may be disposed of in a secure manner at the discretion of the Quality Manager. The date when the hardcopy documents may be disposed of is noted on the Work Order Form. Similarly, copies on disk may be deleted and disks recycled after three years. Refer to retention times below.

The way in which electronic files are backed-up is a matter of individual choice – particularly in a small organisation. Electronic files are backed up on CDs. I use a separate CD for each working day, i.e. Monday to Friday as well as a memory stick for work in progress. A weekly backup is also made and stored off site.

Controlled System Documents

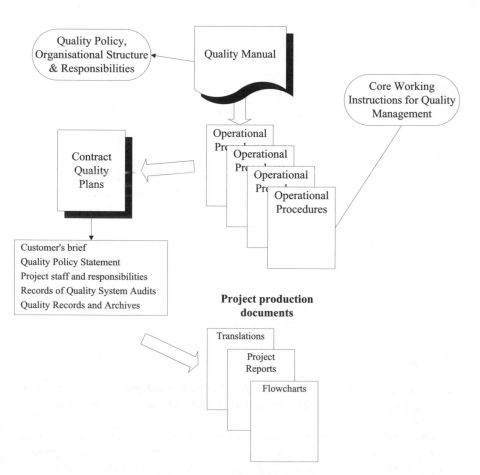

Figure 18.   Controlled system documents

Retention times

All documentation shall be dated so that disposal dates can be calculated. No documentation is destroyed without the authorisation of the Quality Manager. The following table identifies document types and the minimum periods of time during which they are retained after the date of completion. These times shall apply unless a customer requests specifically that other times shall apply.

As defined in the Quality Policy Manual, Job Bag is the term used to describe a plastic folder, cardboard folder or ring binder containing all the information related to a translation assignment or consultancy project.

Type of document	Minimum retention times		Disposal method	
	Hard copies	Electronic copies	Hard copies	Electronic copies
Job bags	3 years	3 years	Secure recycling	Deletion or reformatting
Internal quality audits	3 years	3 years	Secure recycling	Deletion or reformatting
Management reviews	3 years	3 years	Secure recycling	Deletion or reformatting
Accounts records	5 years	5 years	Secure recycling	Deletion or reformatting
Database records	3 years	3 years	Secure recycling	Deletion or reformatting

The Work Order Form is used to record the date when translation or project documentation may be disposed of.

Management commitment

This provides evidence of management commitment to the development and implementation of the company's quality management system and continually improving its effectiveness.

There is a requirement for the Quality Manager to communicate the importance of meeting customer as well as statutory and regulatory requirements to employees and sub-contractors such as freelance translators.

Corporate quality objectives

The general quality objectives for the company are listed in the following table – these complement the quality objectives already considered. Specific objectives for individual projects are discussed with the customer and recorded on the relevant Work Order Form or separately in the Job Bag.

Quality objectives
Understanding of and agreement with the customer on the project's requirements
Producing translations that are suitable for the intended purpose
Enhancement of terminology databases resulting from research during translation projects
Satisfactory completion of pre-delivery checks
Delivery by agreed date and time
Giving feedback to customer that could be beneficial to future projects
Acting on feedback from customers that could contribute to continual improvement

Management reviews

This provides evidence of management reviews of the development and implementation of the company's quality management system and continually improving its effectiveness. The responsibility for the implementation of this procedure is that of the Quality Manager.

The Quality Manager and an Independent Auditor shall carry out twice-yearly reviews of the company's quality system to ensure compliance with the requirements of EN ISO 9001:2000 and the company's stated Quality Policy and objectives. Records of these reviews will be kept by the Quality Manager:

The purpose of this procedure is to:

- review the quality system twice a year
- ensure its continuous suitability and effectiveness in satisfying the requirements of EN ISO 9001:2000 and the stated quality policy
- review methods used to analyse non-conformances detected during the implementation of the company's systems and procedures
- review the steps taken to both study these analyses and to instigate action to prevent further occurrences.

Scope

This procedure is applied to the activities given within this text, and any other notified by the Quality Manager prior to calling a management review meeting.

Responsibilities

This procedure for planning and calling a management review meeting lies with the Quality Manager. The person responsible for producing reports and analyses for a management review meeting is identified by the Quality Manager or the person with this delegated responsibility.

Calling a management review meeting

The Quality Manager is responsible for calling management review meetings at intervals of approximately six months. One week's notice of the date of each review is given by the Quality Manager to the Independent Auditor

The Independent Auditor is responsible for drawing up the agenda in which he includes the reports and analyses which he wishes to be prepared for discussion. The following reports are prepared for presentation at the management review meeting when requested.

Audit report

This is prepared by the Quality Manager and indicates the areas of deviations from the procedures that were discovered during the audits undertaken since the last management review meeting and recommends actions to prevent further instances.

Where there are continuing deviations from the correct operation of the procedures, the report may recommend a study of the procedures in question to improve their effectiveness.

Customer complaints report

This is prepared by the Independent Auditor and indicates the main types of discrepancies discovered by customers as a percentage of the total output from the company and indicates areas where improvements could be made.

Other reports

Where the Quality Manager requires reports other than those given above to be submitted, the content of the report required and the person by whom it is to prepared are notified by the Quality Manager at the time of calling the meeting.

Meeting agenda

The meeting first considers all actions placed at the previous meeting and checks that they are both completed and have proved effective. Where this is not so, the notes record the reasons for this failure and what further action is to take place. The meeting then considers each report in turn together with the recommendations made by the person who prepared the report. Items for consideration are:

- Performance of sub-contractors (freelance translators and other service providers). Training necessary to meet market requirements.
- Changes in legislation and regulations.
- Methods of working.
- Audits.
- Other relevant reports.

Minutes are taken at the meeting either by the Quality Manager or someone appointed to that task; the final recommendations are included in the minutes together with the name[s] of the person[s] who are to implement the recommendations and the timescales by which the activities are to be completed.

Opportunities for improvement

Any error, observation or non-conformance is an opportunity for improvement. If, when performing pre-delivery checks, an error, observation or non-conformance is noted, corrective action is taken to rectify the situation before the work is delivered to the customer. Where necessary, constructive comments are given to the person who performed the work so that note can be taken of the comments thereby ensuring that appropriate preventive action is taken in future.

While it is difficult in some cases to be aware in advance of what errors might arise, forward planning can heighten awareness by anticipating where improvements could be possible. Continuous awareness of the following is maintained to achieve this objective and such items will be included in management review discussion.

Records of the above and any action taken are recorded in a separate ring binder kept for the purpose.

Internal audit

Flowcharts for an internal audit and the preventive and corrective process are given on the following pages.

Internal audit

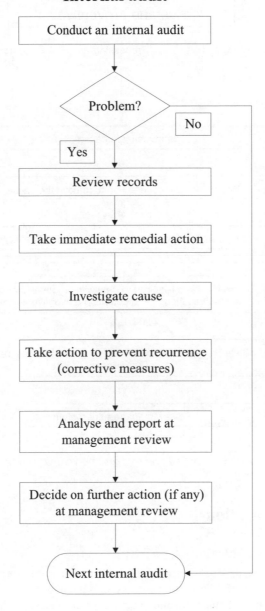

Figure 19.   Internal audit flowchart

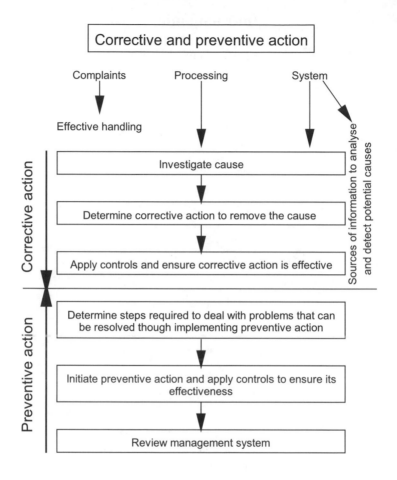

Figure 20. Corrective and preventive action

Product realisation

Introduction

This procedure describes the method by which enquiries and orders received by the company are dealt with. This procedure is designed to ensure that the customer's requirements are fully understood and accepted prior to starting the work on the order or project.

General quality objectives are determined by the intended use for the translation and are described in the following table. These depend of course on what is agreed between the company and the customer. Style and layout are not really a measurement of translation quality but the presentation can often be improved upon.

Unless stated otherwise by the customer it will be assumed that translation is for information only. It is wise not to presume this and ask specifically what the translation will be used for. Specific quality requirements noted by the customer will be recorded on the Work Order Form.

Translation is not a regulated profession, in the United Kingdom at least. Anybody can call themselves a translator but is unlikely to receive work unless competence can be demonstrated. A yardstick in the United Kingdom is that a qualified translator should be a Member of the Institute of Linguists or the Institute of Translation and Interpreting (or equivalent), should have a working knowledge of the subject being translated and at least three years' full-time experience. A trainee translator should work under the supervision of a qualified translator.

Enquiries and requests for pricing information

The responsibility for dealing with enquiries and pricing information lies with the Project Manager or the person to whom this responsibility has been delegated. An offer of a contract shall be declined if the company does not have the resources or skills to meet the customer's requirements.

Costing process and agreement on terms of payment

Costing for an individual contract or project is not provided for regular customers where terms and conditions, including a pricing structure, are agreed in advance unless a particular project warrants such action. Work from other sources will be costed in advance and no work accepted until the cost structure is approved by the customer.

No work should be accepted unless terms of payment have been mutually accepted and agreed. Making a unilateral statement of terms and conditions is of little value except for a basis of discussion. All sums due to the company shall be paid within 30 days following the date of the invoice ('the Settlement Date') and may not be withheld or delayed because of any alleged defects in services supplied. The company reserves the right to charge interest on overdue accounts at the rate of 2% per month compounded monthly to run from the Settlement Date until receipt by the company of the full amount (including any accrued interest).

Late Payment of Commercial Debts (Interest) Act 1998: A User's Guide is used for this purpose.

Confirmation of costing by the customer

Where the customer telephones to accept the costing, the name of the customer representative is noted on the document related to the customer (letter, email or fax). Written confirmation should be requested. When the details of the project are confirmed, these are checked to ensure that the work to be done is the same as that for which the costing was calculated. Where this is not the case, the customer is contacted to resolve the issue.

Order registration

Customer name allocation on the computer network

The Customer is allocated an archive directory identified by the Customer's name once a job is complete. The choice of customer name shall facilitate identification. The job folders relating to a customer's project shall be stored in the relevant sub-directory (e.g. LIVE, or ARCHIVE) according to the state of completion of the work.

Recording details of an order

The necessary details concerning the order are noted in the Job Book against the next available Job Number. The Work Order Form is completed using the information provided by the customer.

The customer's source documentation is stored in the Job Bag. If the job details are too extensive or the documentation is too bulky to fit in the Job Bag, they may be stored separately in a secure manner such as in a ring binder. The same applies in the case of a large project where it would be inefficient to reproduce the job details for each part of the project.

Electronic copies of work received from the customer are stored in the LIVE directory while work is in progress and transferred to the ARCHIVE directory when the work is completed as specified in procedure GSB-Proc 07, Customer Property.

The customer's covering documentation is attached to the Work Order Form and placed with the source document in the Job Bag. Faxed copies of any pertinent documentation or correspondence are also kept in the Job Bag.

Amendment to a contract

If an amendment is made to a contract where a Work Order Form has been raised, but before work on that contract has been commenced, a new offer (quotation) is submitted to the customer for approval. A new contract is made when the customer accepts the revised offer and a revised Work Order Form is raised.

If an amendment is proposed while work is in progress, agreement on the scope and cost of the amended contract is to be agreed with the customer and noted on an amended Work Order Form. An amendment may be noted on the original Work Order Form if the change is minor.

Make sure there is evidence of all correspondence related to the amendment and this is stored in the Job Bag.

Monthly account records for major customers

It may be practical to invoice regular customers on a monthly basis. In this case, all jobs will come under a single job number plus a supplement A, B, C, etc to identify the individual projects. A single monthly invoice will be submitted to the customer but will identify each project by the customer's order or reference number. This is practical and economic if billing a foreign customer and the bank makes a charge for negotiating a cheque from a foreign payee bank.

Reference material

If the project is for translation and the purpose of the translation is stated or the translation requires the use of specific vocabulary or a high degree of consistency, reference material to achieve this shall be requested from the customer or obtained from the company's own resources. Originals of reference material shall be kept in the Job Bag or suitably stored while the work is in progress. When the work is complete, the reference material shall be returned to customer, if so requested, or suitably stored for future reference.

Records

The following information is contained in the Job Bag for work in progress:

a) The Work Order Form.
b) The customer's covering document including the Customer's purchase order and any other documents relevant to the project.
c) The work to be translated or documentation produced for the project.
d) Reference material that is applicable.
e) Project documentation that is undergoing quality control.

Customer focus

This describes how the company ensures that customer requirements are determined and met with the aim of enhancing customer satisfaction.

The procedure also describes the method by which customer complaints are recorded and processed so that corrective and preventive action can be taken.

The forms used in this procedure are the Work Order Form and the Customer Complaint Form. The latter is used to capture information regarding a customer complaint, and details of the investigation into the causes and any compensation or remedial action. Copies of these forms are included in the Forms section of the quality manual.

Quality of the source material

The quality of the source material for translation or the consultancy brief influences the quality of the services provided by the company.

My own experience shows that the translator often needs to carry out pre-editing of the source document before work on it can commence. This is particularly so when computer-aided translation is used. Common faults in the source document are:

- The person who wrote the source text knew what he wanted to say but has not expressed this articulately in what he has written. This problem will be compounded if the source document is to be translated into a number of target languages.
- Inconsistent formatting of the source text that can disrupt translation if, for example, a forced line break is used in a sentence instead of allowing a natural break to occur. Such breaks also occur if a Word file is compiled from a PDF or website text.
- Inconsistent use or no use of document templates. This can occur if several authors contribute to a manual for example.
- The writer is inexperienced in the use of Word or other document formats. Although the layout may appear satisfactory when the source document is printed out, this is not likely to be the case if the sources text in this format is used in a computer-aided translation package to produces target language documents.

An initial assessment is made on receipt of the material and any quality issue noted on the Work Order Form. If there are any issues that cannot be resolved a list of queries is sent to the customer so that any ambiguity or lack of clarity in the source document can be resolved. If there are any outstanding queries that have not been resolved as a response to queries, a comment is attached to the translation or consultancy report when delivered. A copy of this is also kept in the Job Bag.

It is now common practice to use translation tools such as translation memory and terminology management software. To do this successfully it is essential to have the source documentation in an acceptable electronic format. It is also common to send documentation as a PDF document. Make sure this can be easily converted to a format that can be used together with your translation tools.

Benchmarking the company's services

The company's translation services are principally intellectual output, the scope for benchmarking is often limited by factors beyond the company's control:

- The quality of the source text to be translated – the author may not be a native speaker of the source text.
- The inability to talk directly to the source text author.
- Reluctance by the customer to accept constructive criticism on the source text.
- Who or what determines the quality of the output.
- Tangible benchmarks against which services are measured are:
- The number of customer complaints per 100 assignments – justified and unjustified.
- The percentage of deliveries made before or on time.

Consultancy services can be benchmarked in the same manner and, although the output is still essentially intellectual, there is direct contact with the customer and project objectives that can be benchmarked are more tangible.

Benchmarking customers

The principal benchmarks that can be applied to customers are:

- The level of information provided and its impact on the company's production.
  - provision of an order confirmation that includes a purchase order number and delivery date that has been agreed.
  - lack of awareness by the customer of poor source document quality. It is often left to the translator to resolve poor document quality before translation can begin.
  - name of a project manager or contact person to whom queries can be addressed.

Initially your company will have a small number of customers and it will be clearly apparent which customers need reminding to provide the necessary information. This is requested by email a copy of which is kept in the Job Bag.

- Payment discipline by customer and its impact on the company's financial performance.

- compiling a record of invoice dates.
- dates when payments are due.
- dates when payments were made.
- debtor days per customer to identify slow payers.
- average debtor days.

Information on payment discipline is compiled using an Excel spreadsheet or other appropriate software. Invoices are sent at the end of each month with a reminder sent at the end of the subsequent month is payment is not made.

The company sets its own general benchmarks in terms of the following input factors that have a direct effect on output.

- Clarity of source language.
- Use of style sheets.
- Other comments.

The source text is edited and reformatted where appropriate before translation into English to ensure that the quality of the output document complies with the company's own documentation standard. Relevant documentation and correspondence are stored in the Job bag.

Statistics

The gathering of statistical data is academic to a degree but can be used to form an opinion on the quality of the material provided for translation. This can be used to diplomatically point out that the quality of the translation is affected by the quality of the source documentation. There may be systematic errors in the source text whose correction has a beneficial impact on the translated text.

Remember the 'So what?' test before gathering data and compiling statistics that serve no useful or practical purpose.

Customer complaints

A customer complaint is defined as being when a customer declines to accept a given job or requests a discount or other compensation for the job. Some exchanges with customers, especially those with regular customers, when problems can be resolved immediately, may be disregarded but, if in doubt, they should be treated as complaints. This procedure is designed to capture details of all customer complaints in a uniform manner to provide a basis for measures to minimise future complaints.

Recording of complaints

Each customer complaint will be recorded by the Quality Manager who completes a Customer Complaint Form. The Quality Manager will decide whether any immediate action is necessary to assist the customer and, if so, this action will be recorded on the form. If the customer is satisfied with this action, the form should nonetheless be processed further for information and a matter of record.

The Quality Manager will investigate the origin of the complaint by consulting the records of the work performed. The results of the investigation are then recorded on the Customer Complaint Form together with the action taken to prevent recurrence of the problem, and any suggestion for amendment to quality procedures or instructions.

Feedback to the customer

The Managing Director will draft a letter advising the customer of the findings of the investigation and, where appropriate, of compensation offered and action taken to prevent future occurrences.

Records

Copies of all completed customer complaint forms are retained together with all reports, correspondence and notes of conversations pertinent to the investigation.

Purchasing goods and services

Introduction

This describes how purchases of goods and services are made and how sub-contractors are selected. A purchase order with a sequential purchase order number shall be printed for each purchase and stored in a ring binder.

In the case of purchases of goods the procedure is designed to ensure that:

- Where possible, a written purchase order is prepared and sent by post or fax to record what is being purchased, and its cost.
- If goods or services are ordered by telephone using a credit or debit card a written confirmation order is sent by post or fax as soon as possible after the telephone transaction.
- If goods or services are ordered electronically, electronic confirmation of the order by the supplier shall be printed.

In the case of the selection of sub-contractors for services, the procedure is designed to ensure that:

- Correct requirement specifications are prepared prior to engaging or recruiting sub-contractors.
- Structured processing of applications is performed.

To ensure that the company can provide services to meet customer requirements, appropriate sub-contractors will be selected for inclusion on the company's sub-contractor database to complement the resources that the company already has.

The forms used in this procedure are:

a)   Purchase Order Form or printout of purchase record of an electronic purchase.
b)   Work Order Form.
      This form is used to record the precise requirements of work that is sub-contracted.
c)   Sub-contractor Form. This form is used to record:
      - relevant personal information about the sub-contractor.
      - the skills and experience offered by the sub-contractor.
      - the production facilities offered by the sub-contractor.
      - evidence of professional indemnity insurance cover.

Forms used to purchase goods or services must be worded so that the precise requirements of the goods or services covered by the purchase order are clearly stated.

Records

Copies of purchase orders are kept in the Purchase Order File.

Detailed information on sub-contractors is stored in electronic format is compiled and maintained by the Managing Director or the person with the delegated responsibility and records are password-protected to prevent unauthorised access.

The following records on sub-contractors can be stored either in an appropriate ring binder for practical everyday use and reference as well as in a computer database:

a)   Copy of the sub-contractor's profile, CV or résumé, and copies of any qualification documents provided.
b)   Copies of the correspondence between the sub-contractor and the company.
c)   Details of the sub-contractor's specialist experience, and the necessary skills.

Existing records are updated when:

- A sub-contractor or company on the database informs the company of changes to the information held by the company.

- A request is made by the company for updated information from the sub-contractor or company.
- A sub-contractor or company is removed from the records.

Information which indicates that a sub-contractor produces poor quality work may result in the removal of the erring sub-contractor or company from the database. The Managing Director makes the decision whether or not to delete the sub-contractor from the database. The sub-contractor shall be informed of the reason in writing by the Managing Director.

Verification of purchased products

Office equipment and consumables are inspected on receipt to ensure that they meet the specification in the purchase order. In the case of items that do not meet the specification the supplier shall be contacted immediately to resolve the issue. The procedure for this will depend on the terms and conditions and guarantee offered by the supplier.

Consultancy work, such as IT services, that is sub-contracted shall be checked against the project specifications. Any work that does not meet the specifications shall be returned to the sub-contracted consultant for rectification at no further cost. If this is not feasible, the necessary rectification shall be done by the company and the cost of this deducted from the sub-contracted consultant's invoice where appropriate.

Records

Copies of purchase orders are kept in the Purchase Order File.

Production and service provision

This describes how translation and project documentation are produced by the company, and the checking processes that are carried out to verify the adequacy of this work. The procedure also describes how electronic files are managed to ensure compliance with the work order.

While documentation could be defined as a product, it cannot be monitored and measured using physical monitoring or measuring devices.

Identification of customers

Customers are identified by the name of the organisation or an appropriate abbreviation.

Forms

The form used in this procedure is the Work Order Form.

Project documentation

Specific criteria affecting production and delivery of translations

Requirements specified by the customer are noted on the Work Order Form. Criteria that affect the translating and checking operations, and delivery, are:

- Compliance with customer's requirements.
- Source language.
- Target language.
- Description of the translation.
- Purpose for which the translation is intended.
- Delivery date.
- Software.
- Delivery method.

Work flow

All reasonable efforts are made to ensure that the translation work, project documentation and checking work comply with the requirements stated on the Work Order Form.

An electronic job folder is created for each assignment in the LIVE directory and moved to the ARCHIVE directory when the assignment is completed. Associated documentation will be stored in the Job Bag for the assignment.

Checking

Project documentation is checked, read through and edited to ensure that it is suitable for the intended purpose and that the format conforms to customer requirements. The Work Order Form contains lists of pre-delivery checks for translation and editing production to be completed before work is dispatched. The relevant section of the form used when checking translation work is illustrated below. Non-TRADOS translation refers to work where only a paper copy is provided whereas translations made using TRADOS use an electronic copy of the work to be translated.

It may not always be possible to perform in-house checks on all assignments especially if a translation is made into an obscure language. The responsibility for checking shall be agreed with the customer according to the intended use of the translation.

Sub-contracted work

A modified version of the Work Order Form is used for sub-contracted work.

Customer-specific glossaries

Any glossary provided by the customer takes precedence over other glossaries or dictionaries unless it contains a perceived error. In this event, the customer is contacted to resolve the issue.

Equipment

The company's output is essentially intellectual but some equipment is necessary to facilitate the production process and deliver the service or product to the customer. Computer hardware and software, and communications equipment, are kept updated to meet customer requirements.

Records

The completed job bag shall contain the Work Order Form, any correspondence with the customer, the source text, and a copy of the final translation or project report. Where this is not possible, the location of the source, draft or final text shall be recorded in the section of the Work Order Form for project notes and pricing details.

Quality auditing

This details the steps taken within the company to plan and undertake an internal audit programme which not only checks the continuing adherence of the company to its published procedures, but which also allows that improvements can be made from suggestions made as a result of the audit.

This procedure is applied to all the activities carried out by the company which impact upon the quality of the services provided.

Responsibilities

The audit programme is drawn up by and, after agreement by the Managing Director, implemented by an Independent Auditor.

Assistance in carrying out the audits is obtained from others outside of the company who are trained in auditing techniques. For simplicity, only the title Independent Auditor is used in the text.

Forms

Examples of forms used in this procedure are the Audit Plan, the Audit Report Form and the Audit Discrepancy.

Audit planning

An Audit Plan is drawn up by the Independent Auditor to cover the following year's audit activity. This plan, which covers each area of the company at least once during the year in question and carries the names of the persons who will be undertaking each specific audit, is submitted to the Managing Director for his agreement at least two weeks prior to the date of its implementation. The Managing Director checks that the plan covers the whole range of activities, that the auditors named have been suitably trained and that no auditor is auditing an area under their supervision. He then signs the plan to indicate his agreement and returns it to the Independent Auditor.

The Audit Plan can be based on the following:

Audit Plan Function to be audited:						
Date agreed for audit	Person concerned	Quality responsibility	Related procedure	Auditor	Re-audit date (if applicable)	Audit or re-audit completed

Issued by: . . . . (Auditor)
Approved by: . . . . (Managing Director)

In the event that the company has recruited staff by the time an audit is called for, the Independent Auditor issues the agreed plan to include any employee affected by the plan.

Implementation

The Independent Auditor contacts the persons to be audited before the beginning of the month in which the audit is due to agree a date for the audit to take place. This date is noted on the audit plan.

Where the audit cannot take place within the scheduled time period, the Independent

Auditor arranges for the audit to be carried out within the following month and informs the Managing Director of the change. The change is noted on the plan.

If the audit cannot be re-arranged within the month following that within which it was due, the Independent Auditor reports this to the Managing Director who resolves the matter, either by reverting to the original plan, with the permitted month slippage or by agreeing a larger slippage, under which circumstances the Audit Plan is updated by the Independent Auditor and re-issued to the original distribution.

Audit

The planned audits are carried out against both work being undertaken and the records of work carried out since the last audit.

All discrepancies are noted by the Independent Auditor on an Audit Report Form and an Audit Discrepancy Form is filled in for each discrepancy. Towards the conclusion of the audit, the Independent Auditor discusses the findings with the manager of the area under audit and agrees, where this is possible, to remedial action and a time scale. Where this is not possible, the Independent Auditor enters the reasons given onto the Audit Report Form.

The Independent Auditor then discusses areas where the manager of the area considers that improvements to the quality systems in the area under audit could be improved. These are noted by the Independent Auditor on the Audit Report Form.

The Independent Auditor then obtains the responsible person's signature to indicate agreement with the audit findings and completes the Audit Discrepancy Form. The originals of the Audit Report Form and Audit Discrepancy Form are retained by the Independent Auditor whilst copies are given to the person responsible.

Where there is a lack of agreement regarding either the remedial action to be taken or the timing of that action, the matter is referred by the Independent Auditor to the Managing Director who completes the remedial action block of the Audit Report Form and files the form.

An Audit report form can be based on the following:

XYZ Translations Ltd
Audit Report
Activity audited: ....
Person interviewed: ....
Job description: Managing Director ....
Audit date: 5 April 2005 .... Auditor: ....   (name of auditor).
Audit Report Serial No: ....

General Observations

1.   Check procedure for latest issue in both the master manual and the user's copy.
     Master Issue . . . User's Issue . . . Complete? Yes/No
2.   Check the user's knowledge of the procedure.
     Excellent / Good / Fair / Poor / Non-existent
3.   Take samples and check that the procedure is being followed. No. of
     Samples . . .
     All OK / A few random problems / Systematic problem(s).

Wash Up Meeting

This meeting was held between the auditor and the user on . . . .
Has the Audit Report form been completed? Yes/No
Have the discrepancies been agreed? Yes/No/Not applicable
Have recovery actions been planned? Yes/No/Not applicable
Has a date been set for completion? Yes/No/Not applicable

Additional comments

Ref. No.	Clause No.	Non-compliance and observations raised	NC O

NC denotes a non-compliance whereas O denotes an observation.

Re-audit

A re-audit is conducted if a non-compliance is recorded. The Independent Auditor schedules the re-audit dates into the Audit Plan as the requirement to re-audit arises. These re-audits are carried out by the original auditor, except where this is impracticable, and are limited to checking that the agreed remedial actions have been completed. The Independent Auditor notes the completion of the re-audit on the Audit Discrepancy Form.

Records

The following records of audits are retained for a minimum of 3 years at the discretion of the Independent External Auditor.

- Copies of all issues of the Audit Plan.
- Originals of all Audit Reports and any Re-audits.
- Original of all Audit Discrepancy Forms.

Analysis of data and improvement

This procedure is applied to determine, collect and analyse appropriate data to demonstrate the suitability and effectiveness of the quality management system and where continuous improvement can be made. The procedure is also designed to identify the action required to eliminate the cause of nonconformities to prevent recurrence.

Responsibilities

The Quality Manager is responsible for the implementation of this procedure.

The forms used in this procedure are the Work Order Form and the Customer Complaint Form.

Collection of data

Data is compiled from:

- Comments made on the Work Order Form.
- Conformity of product requirements.
- Reports related to specific assignments that are submitted to customers.
- Customer complaints.

Improvement

Improvement is achieved by identifying opportunities identified in the collection of data and determining what corrective action may be required.

Corrective action

Corrective action is taken in the event of any comments or complaints by the customer. This can be in the form of the following:

- Dealing with customer complaints and identifying non-conformances with customer requirements and thus areas for improvement.
- Incorporating suggestions for improvement suggested by the customer.
- Undergoing further training on new software and updates to software already in use such translation management software.
- Purchasing relevant reference books for knowledge improvement on a particular subject.

Records

Records of Work Order Forms and Customer Complaint Forms are retained for a minimum of 3 years.

6 Work Instructions

Work instructions are written to facilitate the understanding and implementation of procedures where this is considered necessary. In essence, procedures state what the organisation does while supplementary instructions state how this is done. Instructions are normally related to a particular procedure. Procedures are often self-evident and instructions are not always necessary.

Two examples are given in this chapter:

- Management of quality documents.
- Instruction regarding enquiries and requests for pricing information.
- Order Registration.

Management of quality documents

Introduction

This instruction describes the management of updates contained in the Active sub-directory in the ISO 9001:2000 electronic document directory.

Identification of documents by file paths and names

A typical file path and name is

    'C:\Quality management\ISO9001_2000\ACTIVE\PROCEDURES\Q-Policy-AOK'

where 'C' is the letter used to identify the drive on which files are stored. 'Quality management\ISO9001_2000' is the directory in which files are stored. The 'ACTIVE' sub-directory indicates that the document is current, the 'Q-Policy' denotes its reference name in the Quality Manual Index whilst the extension .AOK indicates its issue.

Other sub-directories are '**OBSOLETE**' which indicates that the issue is obsolete but is kept as a reference of the previous issue, and '**REVIEW**' which indicates that the document is currently being reviewed or revised.

Method of amendment of ISO9001: 2000 files

- Copy the file to be amended from the '**ACTIVE**' sub-directory to the '**REVIEW**' and '**OBSOLETE**' sub-directories.
- Call up the file to the screen in the '**REVIEW**' sub-directory.
- Incorporate the amendments.
- Change the issue letter in the header of the document to the next letter.
- Save the amended document under the revised file name using the revised issue letter.
- Using the re-indexing facility in Word for Windows, amend the table of contents.
- Once the amendments have been approved by the Managing Director, move the file to the '**ACTIVE**' sub-directory.
- Ensure that the date of issue and date of approval are not different.
- Delete the now obsolete file from the '**ACTIVE**' sub-directory and any previous obsolete file from the '**OBSOLETE**' sub-directory.

A typical sub-directory tree is illustrated on the next page.

Updating the index to documents

Do not update the index until all amendments to the documents are completed and approved. The sequence for updating the index

(reference: C:\Quality Management\ISO9001_2000\ACTIVE\CONTENTS-*OK)

is analogous to that of other quality documents. (*) indicates the issue letter.

Shown on page 95 is a real example that illustrates the section of the computer drive for the sub-directory containing quality procedures.

The flowchart for document control is shown in Figure 21.

Instruction regarding enquiries and requests for pricing information

Unless an enquiry comes from an established customer, it is unwise to provide pricing information without full knowledge of the work to be done. An enquirer should be asked to provide at least a sample of the work to be done and the scope of the work.

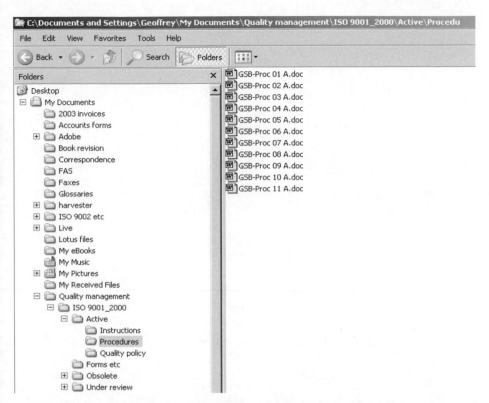

Pricing information shall be offered only if the enquirer is judged to be serious and genuine. While some enquirers may not wish to identify themselves immediately for commercial reasons, other enquiries may be from those wishing to gain commercial advantage from knowing the company's pricing structure. A polite refusal should be given to the latter.

An estimate is provided if the customer provides sample pages of the work to be translated or an outline of the project's scope. A quotation is provided only on sight of the complete documentation or a statement on the scope of the project. If there is any doubt about the scope of the work to be done, a meeting shall be requested in order to reach agreement. The process is encapsulated in the flowchart shown in Figure 22.

The process of considering and criteria for accepting an offer of work are encapsulated in Figure 23.

Written confirmation shall be requested from a new customer, for a complex project, or from a customer known for changing what has already been agreed.

Creditworthiness is judged by the known reputation of the potential customer or by requesting two commercial references in the case of unknown enquirers.

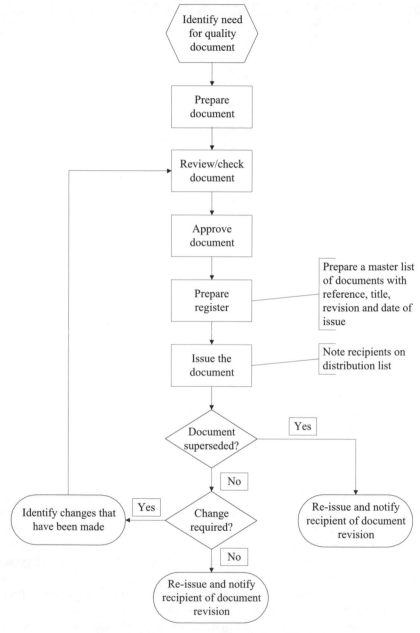

Figure 21. Quality document control flowchart

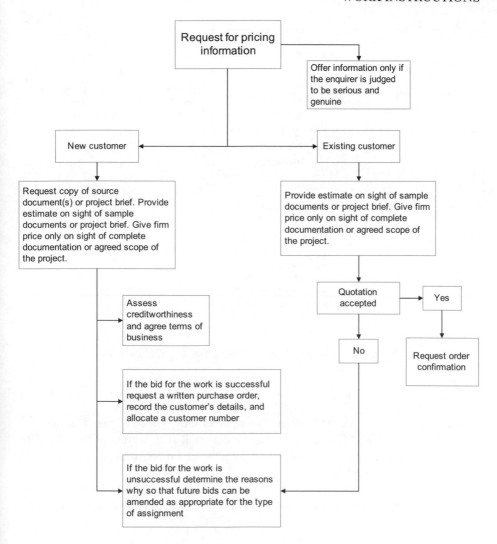

Figure 22. Order acceptance flowchart

Terms of business must be agreed before accepting work. These are normally payment no later than 30 days after the date of invoice.

On receipt of sample pages, the cost of the work will be estimated. A quotation is provided only on receipt of the complete documentation. If necessary, suitable sub-

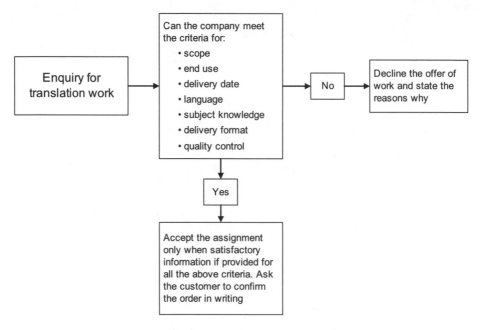

Figure 23. The process of considering an offer of work

contractors are also contacted to determine whether they will be available at the time required. Once availability is ascertained, the customer is then informed of the price and any other pertinent information, either by letter or by fax, whichever is the more convenient for the customer.

A copy of the document containing the costing is filed in the quotations file. The information is transferred to the Work Order Form if the quotation results in an order for work.

Order registration

Once an order is received, brief details are noted in the Job Book. The information shall be legible and unambiguous. The following shall be noted:

- **Date** – the date when the order is received.
- **Job Number** – how you structure this depends on the structure of you business. If a customer sends several assignments during a particular month, a single job

number shall be used and each individual assignment identified by the job number plus a suffix, e.g. 1042A, 1042B, 1042C etc. according to the number of assignments sent. In this case a single invoice for the month is submitted and specifies the jobs included in that invoice. A production record can be maintained as an Excel file but, for the purposes of ISO9001, this is not a controlled document.

- **Type of work** – the type of work is identified by T for translation, C for consultancy assignment, or other designation.
- **Customer Name** – this should contain sufficient information to identify the customer.
- **Description** – sufficient information to describe the work.
- **Date Completed.** – the date when the work is completed and delivered to the customer. The electronic version of the Job Bag is transferred to the Archive file once the job has been invoiced.

The Work Order Form is completed using this information plus other details that are relevant to the work.

Any customer's covering documentation is attached part and placed with the source document in the Job Bag. Faxed copies are also kept in the Job Bag.

7 Managing Human Resources

The company must ensure that it has the appropriate human resources for any service that it offers. If additional resources required are beyond those available at the time of bidding, and there is insufficient time to recruit either staff or freelance resources, the project should be politely declined and an explanation given as to why.

Staff recruitment

The decision to recruit a member of staff is a major commitment and should not be taken without careful consideration. It implies responsibilities for you as an employer to provide a place of work and to ensure that training and continuous development are offered to the prospective employee. Recruiting a member of staff is a long-term commitment. There needs to be a sustainable volume of work otherwise it is better to resolve resources demands by sub-contracting work.

As an employer you are responsible for a significant part of an employee's life. It also means that you must be able to offer the skills and experience appropriate for the job being offered. An interview should not be a one-sided affair. You should be interviewing a prospective employer to ensure that the position being offered is what you want. This is why an interview should be conducted carefully, dispassionately and considerately.

When the need to employ staff arises, the selection and appointment of such staff will be undertaken by the appropriate manager (or the person with delegated responsibility). Qualifications, training and experience will form the basis of the selection and appointment process.

Most interviewees are honest about their capabilities but, exceptionally, a candidate may perform admirably during an interview but is unable to do what is required in practice. Short-listed candidates should be given a practical test on site and under realistic conditions. If interviews do not produce the calibre of candidate required, consider whether appropriate training should be provided. If not, do not accept second best. Re-advertise or reconsider whether the position can be filled using other resources.

The validity of all qualifications should be checked. References should be contacted only when permission to do so is given by the candidate
A model interview record is given in Appendix 2.

The recruitment process

Assuming that you want to develop beyond the capacity of your original resources you will have to make the decision to recruit staff. This is a major step for a fledgling organisation since if you employ staff you will have additional fixed overheads that have to be paid for. Initially you will probably recruit administration and quality control resources and possibly on a part time basis. As the volume of work increases you may decide to employ staff translators/checkers to meet additional customer demands. The following profitability graph shows a point when employing a staff translator can be profitable in terms of variable and fixed costs.

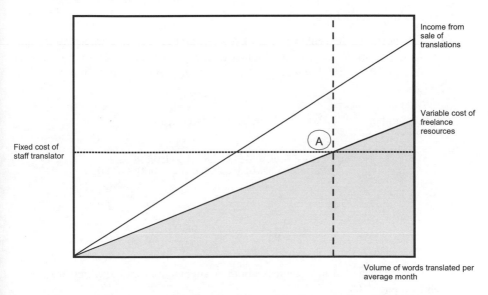

Figure 24.   Comparison of profitability of freelance and staff translators

The point (A) where costs break-even is when the level of production is such that the variable costs of freelance translation is the same as or greater than the fixed cost of an in-house translator. The calculation is based on the following assumptions where the figures are taken as examples. These will depend on the company's prices and costs and do not allow for sickness or other absence.

- A staff translator works effectively for 6 hours a day and produces 340 words an hour of finished text ready for delivery (around 2000 words). This production rate is based on working under ideal conditions. It is optimistic to consider that this is a sustainable rate.
- There is an average of 18.75 working days in a month (allows 25 days holidays plus 10 days public holidays). A translator's average monthly production will be around 37,500 words.
- If we assume that these translations are sold at an average of GBP 120/1000 words giving a gross monthly income of GBP 4,500.
- The monthly fixed cost of a staff translator is estimated at GBP 3,300 (includes project administration, salary, payroll tax, office facilities etc.)
- These figures mean that a staff translator, if fully occupied in translation production, will generate a net income of around GBP 1,000 month giving a profit ratio of around 36%.

Corresponding figures for a freelance are:

- Variable costs for the same volume of words purchased from a freelance translator (including in-house project administration, quality control etc) are estimated at around GBP 95/1000 words or GBP 3,560 per giving a profit ratio of around 21%.

If x is the number of 1000 words, x can be calculated from:

$$x = \frac{\text{monthly cost of staff translator}}{\text{variable cost of freelance (per 1000 words)}}$$

or

$$x = \frac{3,300}{95} = 34,740 \text{ words}$$

There are benefits and disadvantages of both arrangements some of which are shown in the table on page 103.
You should consider how you are going to select and train staff and should therefore have a procedure designed to ensure that:

- Correct job specifications are prepared prior to advertising for and recruiting staff.
- Appropriate training is planned (and later implemented).
- Appropriate human resources are recruited.
- Skills are developed so that the company can provide services to meet customer requirements.

	Staff translators	Freelance translators
Benefits	• Working hours are regulated and work can be timetabled and monitored with reasonable certainty. • Continuous personal development can be planned and tracked. • Immediate communication between translator and project manager/customer. • Staff translators can carry out quality control on each other's work and that of freelance translators.	• The company is charged only for the work agreed. • The freelance may consider working unsocial hours if appropriately rewarded. • Having a choice of freelances enhances the range of languages and subjects that can be offered to customers.
Disadvantages	• Production capacity may be compromised if a translator is off sick for any length of time. • The costs of short-term absence through sickness, medical appointments etc. are borne by the company. • Relying solely on staff translators restricts what can be offered to customers.	• Availability is not always guaranteed since freelances work for several customers. • Queries to customers are usually relayed through project manager and quality gaps could arise. • A freelance works in isolation and seldom has the opportunity to pass work to colleagues for quality control (proof-reading your own work is difficult).

Advertising a staff position

If suitable candidates cannot be approached through personal contacts, a position could be advertised in the local or national press, or in an appropriate professional journal.

Certain guidelines should be followed when composing newspaper adverts for recruiting staff. Adverts are an opportunity for promoting the company as well as advertising the vacancy. Make sure that the visual impact of the advert is as strong as possible. The following information should be included:

Brief introduction	Confirms that your organisation is a well-established and quality-minded company.
Title of position being offered	This should be worded appropriately to attract the right calibre of staff you are looking for.
More detailed description of the position	The description should identify the principal duties and the qualifications required to do the job efficiently. This section should also list the vocational and IT skills required.
Working conditions etc.	Brief details of the working environment, personal development prospects and working hours.

Contact person	Name of the person from whom application forms are available or to whom applications shall be sent, and who is able to answer queries from any potential applicant.
Address details	This could include your website address so that potential applicants can find out more about your organisation. This can also act as a filter. State the address to which written applications must be sent. The words NO AGENCIES are included unless responses from agencies are solicited.
Corporate credentials	Include any logos from professional organisations of which you or your organisation is a member that increase the potential impact of the advertisement.

Interview process

- Acknowledge and file all responses to advertisements within five working days.
- Once candidates for interview have been short-listed send polite letters of rejection within five working days to unsuccessful applicants.
- Write letters to take up references where applicants have sanctioned this. In some cases it may be appropriate to contact referees by telephone since they will be more inclined to admit sensitive details off the record.
- File copies of references and notes from telephone conversations.
- Write letters inviting applicants to attend interview. Request any further supporting evidence that may be required. Advise the candidate that he will be asked to take a practical test to demonstrate his competence.
- For the sake of expediency it may be appropriate on occasions to telephone the applicant and extend an invitation to attend an interview.

Interview checklist

Agree on an acceptable suitable date and time for the interview. When inviting a translation candidate for an interview, make sure that the interviewee is aware that he will be required to carry out a translation test as part of the interview assessment process. Other staff candidates should be tested to ensure that they have adequate skills in the software they will be required to use.

In addition to making the interview candidate at feel at ease by offering refreshment and other comforts make sure that the candidate is not kept waiting. If you are unavoidably detained, make sure that somebody has been delegated to look after the interviewee in your absence.

1.   Prepare appropriate facilities and make sure resources (including reference material)

are available for any candidates to perform a test translation or other work for assessment.

2. Provide the candidate with an opportunity to meet the staff he will be working with while being given a tour of the workplace. This will make the candidate feel welcome and at ease in an unfamiliar environment. The scope of the tour will be confined to areas that do not compromise the organisation's confidentiality.

3. Make sure the appropriate documentation is available for the interview:
    - Application Form submitted by the candidate.
    - Job Interview Record.
    - Job Description.
    - Other supporting documents.

4. Ensure that you are adequately prepared for carrying out the interview.

5. Use a job description to ensure that any specific knowledge, skills, and experience sought are appropriate to the job and not inferior to the minimum necessary for the job to be carried out effectively.

6. Ask open questions and clarify any doubts you might have about the candidate's application or qualifications. Make clear and concise notes that you can refer to after the interview.

7. Interviewing is a two-way process since interviewees should also be interviewing you to decide whether or not your organisation offers what the interviewee is looking for.

8. Offer reimbursement for travelling costs before the interviewee leaves.

Correspondence after interviews

- Make a written offer to the preferred candidate. If there is no preferred candidate consider re-advertising rather than accepting a candidate who does not meet requirements.
- When written confirmation of acceptance of an offer is received, notify the remaining unsuccessful candidates of the decision. Be impartial in your responses and provide constructive assessments of the test translations made by interviewees.

Records

- Destroy all correspondence relating to unsuccessful candidates except from applicants who are considered worthy of consideration in the future.
- File and lock away all other correspondence.

Advertising through recruitment agencies

If an inadequate response is received through newspaper advertising it may be appropriate to commission a recruitment agency to recruit staff. Get an agency representative to visit you so that he is given a comprehensive introduction to your organisation, is fully briefed and is able to offer the calibre of staff you are looking for. Provide the representative with the following information:

- A comprehensive job description so that appropriate candidates can be presented by the agency.
- Any specific terms appropriate to the position being recruited.
- The organisation's corporate literature and company profile or reference to the organisation's website.

A recruitment agency has two objectives:

1) To place a candidate who is on their database.
2) To bill you for the service they provide – the fee is usually a percentage of the first year's salary offered to the candidate.

Don't just accept the first candidate offered but request further interviewees until you find the person you want.

Summer students

Students are becoming more adept at proactively approaching potential employers and offering their services as a way of gaining work experience and professional credibility. The following appeared originally in 'A Practical Guide for Translators' (see Reading list on page 135). It appears here in a modified format.

On pages 107 and 108 is an example of a memo issued with an eight-week programme designed to offer a French university student broad exposure to what goes on in a translation company. It also shows how staff members should be involved and support the student

There are, of course, routine tasks that everybody has to do – these include photocopying and word counting. Make sure that a structured programme is offered, that the student is not being used as a dogsbody, and that he derives benefit from the experience.

Since the company offering the placement will incur costs as a result, not least by providing a member of staff as a supervisor and facilities, a student on placement should not expect to receive a salary even though some discretionary payment may be made. The student can gain considerable benefit through meeting experienced practitioners and seeing what goes on in a translation company. The student may decide after the placement that translation is not for him. He then has a chance of redirecting his studies.

Summer placement programme – Richard X

Distribution: All staff

Introduction

The purpose of this Summer placement with XYZ Limited is to provide Richard with a broad exposure to the different operations that are performed at a translation company, and an appreciation that being a translator is a very demanding and exacting profession.

Where applicable, the relevant procedures in XYZ's Quality Manual shall be studied in parallel with the different operations, e.g. XYZ/OPS 02 Translator Selection. Comments should be invited on the comprehensibility of the procedures by an uninitiated reader.

Richard will be here from 1 July – 31 August and his supervisor will be FS. This responsibility will be shared with those looking after Richard in the various sections:

- Production coordination – KN
- Proof-reading and quality control – AL and SM
- Administration – JA
- Freelance translator assessment – MS

I'm sure that all members of staff will do their best to make Richard's stay with us both enjoyable and rewarding.

Information to be provided

Information pack about the company to include:

- XYZ's leaflet in English
- Organisation chart
- Copy of 'A Practical Guide for Translators'

Other information will be provided by the various section supervisors.

Translation, proof-reading and editing
- Familiarisation with the C-C project.
- Reviewing XYZ's presentation slides in French
- checking overheads produced by SH. Emphasis on the importance of accuracy.

Read through SRDE manual in French and English to provide a concept of what is involved.

- One-to-one session with SM on the different types of proof reading:
  * proof-reading marks as per BS 5261
  * scan-check for information purposes only
  * full checking
  * checking for publication
  * checking documents for legal certification

(continued

Database management
MS will provide an introduction to database management and the way freelance translators are selected. The emphasis shall be on stringent criteria for selection and the way in which the information is managed.
KN will supervise an introduction to the way database management is used as a tool in production coordination.

Project management
JA and KN will provide an introduction to project management and its significance as a key factor for success in a translation company. This will include:

- Familiarisation with the quality control and project management aspects of Customer XXXX
- Project management of Customer YYYY assignments
- Administration associated with an assignment from initial inquiry to when the work is sent to the customer
- Use of different communication media such as fax and electronic mail.

Library and information retrieval
A familiarisation with XYZ's library and its collection of dictionaries, glossaries, text books, reference books, company literature and past translations will be provided by HJ.

General administration
Richard will be delegated routine administration tasks such as photocopying and word counting.

Customer visits
If the opportunity arises, and if deemed relevant, Richard will be invited to accompany members of staff on customer visits as an observer. Customers will be contacted in advance to seek their approval.

Weekly reviews
FS will hold weekly reviews with Richard to assess progress and seek solutions to any problems.

Place, date

The sponsoring company has the opportunity to learn what is being offered to students and perhaps have an influence on what students are taught. It also provides an opportunity for the company to gain market exposure as a consequence of its altruistic endeavours.

Staff training and development

It is worthwhile considering the difference between education and training. It is expected that a new employee will have the appropriate education for the work to be done and that training is a continuous acquisition of vocational skills.

Education typically takes place in a classroom and involves a transfer of knowledge through the use of formal methods such as lectures and directed discussion. Participants learn new and relevant information, but the acquisition of new skills and competences, designed to enhance profitability or quality is usually not the intended outcome; i.e. their ability to actually do something new is often not exploited. In other words, knowing about a skill is not the same as being skilful.

Training, on the other hand, typically entails personal involvement, commitment, and experiential gains. Training involves learning by doing. Competence, much more than knowledge, constitutes real power. True training occurs when skills that can be measurably defined are enhanced until the competence level is visibly enhanced. Training aims to provide employees with proficiency in the execution of given tasks. The outcomes of training should be tangible, in that they should complement and support the company's financial stability.

It is unlikely that a prospective employee has precisely the attributes and skills required by a job. Initial induction and training should therefore be provided so that a job can be done to mutual satisfaction. Long-term personal development and training to meet changing needs and requirements should be discussed according to the demands of the work done and during regular appraisals between the employee and manager.

Some would argue against training with the pessimistic view that as soon as anybody has received training they will then use this experience and skills they have learned to seek a better position. I take the view that it is better to have a trained person for six months than an untrained person for, say, two years. The latter will not perform optimally and this could lead to long-term disbenefits for the company.

Staff regulations

Initially when a company is formed it is full of revolutionary zeal and issues such as staff regulations seem bureaucratic, unnecessary and distant. Such regulations are, however, designed to protect employer and employee alike. It is better to have regulations in place rather than trying to sort out issues at a later date when there are no such regulations that determine what, when and how. They also set the tone and project a serious image from the outset.

A model for staff regulations is given in Appendix 3.

Engaging freelance staff

Criteria for selecting suppliers

Goods are purchased from suppliers and sub-contractors who, in the opinion of the Quality Manager or person with delegated responsibility, are appropriate for the goods supplied.

Applications in response to advertising or unsolicited applications from sub-contractors should be considered for processing only if there is a requirement for additional sub-contractors. Preference will be given to sub-contractors who are suitably qualified through membership of a reputable professional organisation and has an established reputation. The following criteria are used as a guide for selection:

a) Does the sub-contractor have the relevant professional qualifications and experience in the appropriate discipline or is he a member of a recognised professional association?

b) Does the sub-contractor have at least three years' full time, or equivalent part time, experience in the appropriate discipline?

c) Does the sub-contractor have the appropriate resources such as hardware and software to produce and deliver the documentation that may be required by a project.

An applicant shall provide evidence to show that he is covered by adequate professional indemnity insurance.

Freelance resources are indispensable to translation agencies since, in most cases, the latter would not remain in business or be successful without them. There is a mutual dependency between agencies and freelances and the working relationship between them needs to be nurtured and developed. There are still agencies that exploit freelances but these are in a small minority.

It is not difficult to attract freelance resources and the art of managing these is to look at developing them in the long term. This is not just being altruistic but an investment in skills. Having worked on both sides of the divide I have seen how respect and appreciation can develop loyal and skilled resources that, as an agency, you know you can depend on.

If you have a web site you will regularly receives solicitations by email. These can be quickly acknowledged and responded to by using the Reply facility in your email programme. Any enquiries that are considered of interest can be forwarded to the appropriate person while others can be deleted once acknowledged.

If you advertise in the Yellow Pages or one of the professional translator journals such as The Linguist or the ITI Bulletin to recruit freelances to you will be overwhelmed with applications from people seeking work. The important consideration is to compose any advert to attract the language/subject combinations you need for your company's planned development and be clear about the qualifications and experience you expect. If you have an advert in the Yellow Pages or have a website you will receive unsolicited applications whether you like it or not. Adverts will also attract enquiries from would-be translators seeing advice – you will also have to consider how you are going to deal with these.

More and more translation agencies are making use of internet facilities to recruit freelance resources and invite freelances to accept or bid for work. While this is a practical and passive way of working, it de-personalises contact with the translator.

Assessing and processing applications in response to advertising

Since you have invited replies the first thing to do is to send an acknowledgement. If you don't you will be branded as being impolite and this will not enhance your corporate reputation. It takes a long time to build up a good reputation but this can quickly be tarnished by unintentional lack of consideration. The following suggests a process for professional recruitment.

It's all very well deciding that you plan to recruit freelance translators. Some agencies advertise that they have thousands of translators on their books – this may sound impressive in advertising but how are these resources managed? Just having a large database for no purpose is disheartening for those who are never used and a waste of administration time in updating and managing a large database.

Recruit only the resources you know are needed for present requirements and what are envisaged in your marketing plan. Be quite specific in your advertising so that you can easily filter out the applications that do not meet the appropriate criteria. It is a simple matter to reply and politely reject such applications.

Processing suitable applications from sub-contractors

All solicited applications should be acknowledged in writing within five working days. All suitable but unsolicited applications should be acknowledged within two working weeks. All correspondence and documentation related to the unsuccessful applicants shall be destroyed as soon an acknowledgement has been posted.

Formal qualifications shall be verified by asking the applicant to provide photocopies of any qualifications that are claimed.

Details of suitable applicants shall be entered on the database. The applicant is allocated a database number which then becomes his sub-contractor number.

While the organisation is not obliged to respond to unsolicited approaches, the politeness of sending a response stating that the company has no requirements at present that match the applicant's skills. Do not say that you will keep details on file if you have no anticipated requirement and you have no intention of doing so. A polite reply will be remembered and is good PR.

Have a policy of replying to all solicited applications within 10 working days. Those that warrant further consideration should be examined to determine if further information is required and to request such information from the applicant.

Always ask for evidence of qualifications. It sounds amazing that anybody would try and pretend they have the qualifications for a job when it would be quickly apparent

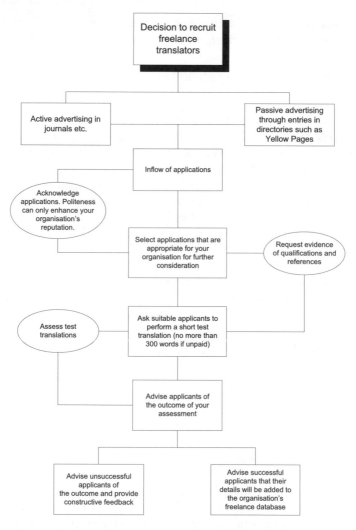

Figure 25. Dealing with applications from freelance translators

that the person concerned is not competent. I have, in the past, taken a great number of enquiries from would-be freelances and have been given responses to questions about qualifications that ranged from the naïve to the dishonest. One enquirer stated that he held a diploma from the Institute of Translation and Interpreting and when I probed further and revealed that I was a founder member and Fellow of the Institute and was not aware that the Institute awards a diploma his response was, '*Well, it must have been from some other organisation*'. I politely suggested that it would be counterproductive to continue the conversation.

By asking for evidence of qualifications you are demonstrating that you are running a professional organisation and that you take quality seriously.

Test translations

How you test the skills of a candidate to be included on your database is a sensitive subject. The applicant may feel that he has the appropriate skills and formal qualifications that you demand and that being asked to do a test translation is to put these in doubt. Some agencies pay for short test translation. Another way of testing a candidate is to give them a short live assignment, for which he is paid, and have it checked (anonymously) by a second translator. This will allow you to assess the candidate under realistic commercial conditions.

Test translations are a sticky point with some freelances and I suppose the only response to any reluctance to do a test translation is 'Would you buy a car without test driving it?' I am not averse to doing a test translation of no more than 300 words (that's if I'm interested in doing work for the potential customer) since this gives me the opportunity to demonstrate my competence and, not unimportantly, shows that the agency or customer I would like to work for is making sure that the freelance engaged for an assignment is competent. If a customer or agency wants more than 300 words done free of charge I ask for payment or suggest that 300 words ought to be sufficient to assess my competence.

I have often done test translations in response to requests and I always state than critical and constructive assessment is always welcome. One potential work provider also required that the test translation be done at a specific time of day with the test text to be sent just before the allotted time and that the translation be returned within a given time! I imagine this was a requirement for testing whether urgent translations could be done within strict time parameters.

A test translation is mandatory if you are considering employing a staff translator. The test must be must be conducted at your premises so that you are able to judge whether the candidate is able to work in your office environment under realistic conditions and has the skills required. Again a further example is worth quoting. I once interviewed a candidate who had what appeared to have a suitable CV and experience. The candidate had to travel a long distance to attend an interview and it was agreed, because of time constraints, that he would carry out a test translation at home after the interview providing he submitted a written statement when returning the translation that the work was his own. The translation arrived in the post a few days later, was found to be acceptable, and he was offered the position. When he started work it was soon discovered that his keyboarding and computer skills were almost non-existent and that, despite coaching, it was obvious that these skills would not improve. Regrettably his period of employment was quickly curtailed. Not only did we fail to get a suitable candidate, we also incurred financial costs and lost time in the process.

Freelance database management

One of the issues that you need to consider carefully before you start the process is that you will need to process the information in a manner that is beneficial to the organisation. You should include on your database only applications from people that you will be able to use to meet your corporate objectives. There is no point in having a massive database of freelances that you will not use and which creates unnecessary bureaucracy. One example of an agency claim in Yellow Pages advertising states that the agency has 'a database of 8000 translators' – managing such a volume is a considerable task let alone carrying out any form of assessment apart from accepting what the freelance states in his personal presentation. There is of course the argument that the freelance can be tested if a need arises.

Remember that you will also need to be registered with the Data Protection Register (or equivalent body) if you intend storing personal data within your organisation.

Terms of business

Once you have agreed to use a freelance translator there should be mutually-agreed terms of business. The ITI has model terms that can be adapted and applied. Your working relationship with freelance translators must also include how you might resolve complaints the most common of which are:

Late delivery – A freelance should have access to the work to be translated before accepting an assignment so that a realistic delivery date can be agreed. Encourage freelances to report any reason why a translation could be delayed since unforeseen circumstances can arise. A common cause of delay is when queries are relayed to the end customer who takes time to respond thus making it difficult or impossible to meet the deadline originally agreed.

Translation does not meet requirements – The freelance must be given comprehensive information on how the translation is to be presented. Unless stated otherwise, the translation will be provided for information purposes only.

Establishing credentials

While no formal qualifications are required to work as a translator, it is common practice for all buyers of translation services and users of in-house resources to demand a level of formal qualification. Certainly most translation agencies demand membership of an appropriate professional organisation as a level of recognised competence. To give an example, the following are the requirements for full membership (MITI) of the Institute of Translation and Interpreting.

Requirements for qualified membership

1. A minimum age of 25 years.
2. A first degree or postgraduate qualification in a relevant subject or a corresponding qualification accepted by ITI.
3. Recommendation regarding ability and good repute by at least three persons for translators, interpreters and lecturers (two professional and one character), and five for conference interpreters (see below).
4. Recent professional experience.
5. Submission of a full CV.

For translators:

A minimum of five years' full-time work (or a correspondingly longer period part-time) and successful assessment of work or a Pass in the ITI Membership Examination; alternatively, three years' full-time (or correspondingly longer part-time), plus a Pass in the ITI Membership Examination, unless the applicant can satisfy the Admissions Committee that there are exceptionally strong grounds for exemption. Submission of a breakdown giving a clear overview of the volume of work completed in the last 3 to 5 years.

For interpreters:

A minimum of 200 days over a period of five years plus a successful Assessment Interview; alternatively, a minimum of 120 days over a period of three years plus a Pass in the ITI Membership Examination, and/or successful Assessment Interview.

Similar criteria are applied by other translator organisations.

Professional development

It is now recognised that merely becoming qualified is just the initial stage in establishing professional credentials. Working as a professional translator involves lifelong learning in a number of disciplines of which the following are perhaps the most important:

- Subject knowledge.
- Software and hardware proficiency.
- Expertise improvement.
- Customer relations.
- Business skills.

These are encapsulated in Figure 1.

The Institute of Translation and interpreting offers a course on continuous personal development at various locations in the UK. The following is an example showing course content and the different modules that can be chosen separately.

Module 1: Language skills

Participants will be encouraged to consider mother tongue skills as an essential part of their toolkit. The module will cover writing, editing and techniques for improving revision accuracy.

Topics to include: maintaining TL (mother tongue) skills; keeping up with the SL; grammar & spellchecking; revision, editing, proofreading, abstracting; writing styles – writing for particular purposes; terminology handling; using dictionaries and reference books; handling specialised texts.

Module 2: Subject knowledge

Participants will gain an appreciation of what specialisation is, how to research a special subject and how to maintain their knowledge in financial, legal, medical, political and technical fields.

Topics to include: how to research a special subject; sources of specialised information; information resources; efficient use of the Internet; organising your own information.

Module 3: Business practice

Experts in accounting, banking and taxation will explain the essentials of setting up a new business. Participants will be guided in the development of a business plan and will tackle such issues as rates and pricing.

Topics to include: setting up a new business; cash flow – bank loans; banking, accounts & taxation (income tax, VAT); invoicing, late payers; overseas payments; project management; rates, dealing with clients; local business support; ITI Standard Terms of Business and other support from ITI.

Module 4: IT and the Internet

Participants will be guided in the software and Internet skills needed by professional translators, as well as advanced word-processing techniques, file transfer and translation technology.

Topics to include: essential software and ways of maximising its potential; keeping your system up and running; dealing with file formats; myths and truths about the Internet; using e-mail; virus and firewall software; translation memory and other translation technology; voice input for translation.

Module 5: Personal development

Participants will learn how to look after their most important asset: themselves. They will learn how to organise their time, how to minimise stress, and how to meet professional standards.

Topics to include: ergonomics, fitness and nutrition; voice care for translators and interpreters; assertiveness, self-promotion; negotiating skills and interview technique; time management; professional standards and ethics.

Procedures for managing external resources

Purchasing

This quality procedure describes the method by which purchases or goods and services are made and how sub-contractors (in addition to freelance translators) are selected.

A purchase order with a sequential purchase order number shall be printed for each purchase and stored in a ring binder.

In the case of purchases of goods the procedure is designed to ensure:

- That, where possible, a written purchase order is prepared and sent by post or fax to record what is being purchased, and its cost.
- That if goods or services are ordered by telephone using a credit or debit card a written confirmation order is sent by post or fax as soon as possible after the telephone transaction.
- That if goods or services are ordered electronically, electronic confirmation of the order by the supplier shall be printed.

In the case of the selection of sub-contractors for services, the procedure is designed to ensure:

- That correct requirement specifications are prepared prior to engaging or recruiting sub-contractors.
- That structured processing of applications is performed.

To ensure that the company can provide services to meet customer requirements, appropriate sub-contractors will be selected for inclusion on the company's sub-contractor database to complement the resources provided by the company.

Forms

The forms used in this procedure for managing external resources are:

a) Purchase Order Form P/3 or printout of purchase record of electronic purchase.
b)Work Order Form P/2.
   This form is used to record the precise requirements of work that is sub-contracted.
c) Sub-contractor Record, Form D/1. This form is used to record:
   - relevant personal information about the sub-contractor.
   - the skills and experience offered by the sub-contractor.
   - the production facilities offered by the sub-contractor.
   - evidence of professional indemnity insurance cover.

Forms used to purchase goods or services must be worded so that the precise requirements of the goods or services covered by the purchase order are clearly stated.

Criteria for selection

Goods and services are purchased from suppliers and sub-contractors who, in the opinion of the Managing Director, are appropriate for the goods supplied.

Applications in response to advertising or unsolicited applications from sub-contractors will be considered for processing only if there is a requirement for additional sub-contractors. Preference will be given to sub-contractors who are suitably qualified through membership of a reputable professional organisation or if the sub-contractor is known personally by the Managing Director and has an established reputation. The following criteria are used as a guide for selection:

- Does the sub-contractor have the relevant professional qualifications and experience in the appropriate discipline or is he a member of a recognised professional association?
- Does the sub-contractor have at least three years' full time, or equivalent part time, experience in the appropriate discipline?
- Does the sub-contractor have the appropriate resources such as hardware and software to produce and deliver the documentation that may be required by a project.
- An applicant shall provide a copy to show that he is covered by adequate professional indemnity insurance.

Processing of suitable applications from sub-contractors

All solicited applications shall be acknowledged in writing within five working days. All suitable but unsolicited applications shall be acknowledged within two working weeks. All correspondence and documentation related to the unsuccessful applicants shall be destroyed as soon an acknowledgement has been posted.

Formal qualifications shall be verified by asking the applicant to provide photocopies of any qualifications that are claimed.

Details of suitable applicants shall be entered on the database. The applicant is allocated a database number which then becomes his sub-contractor number.

Physical resources

The company shall ensure that it has the appropriate physical resources. Such resources include the following:

- Computer hardware and software, and peripheral equipment.
- Telecommunications equipment to facilitate verbal communication and electronic file transfer.
- Reference material for translation projects.
- Office space and furniture that provides an optimum working environment.

The company has these resources and they will be upgraded when appropriate to meet customer requirements.

8 Customer Relations

Customer misconceptions

When discussing the provision of translation services with a potential customer it is best to assume that the customer has little or no knowledge of what is required. Do not treat the customer in a patronising manner but offer advice and guidance as appropriate. Uninformed customer expectations can be unrealistic. Finding out what a potential customer knows about translation needs to be done with a degree of diplomacy and without being patronising. The following are examples of typical misconceptions:

- The translator can work into a number of languages none of which is his mother tongue.
- The translator is able to tackle all subjects without support or specialist knowledge.
- The translator will be able to handle all software formats – Microsoft Word, Microsoft Excel, Powerpoint, Framemaker, Visio, Pagemaker, PDF and so on.
- The translator can work 24 hours a day and can produce a perfect translation at the first attempt without having to resolve queries with the customer.
- The translator is available at any time and is prepared to work unsocial hours for no additional reward.
- Checking and proofreading take no time at all.
- The translator is happy to accept a very modest fee and the work is its own reward.

Customer education

Fortunately the majority of customers are informed but a great deal of customer education is often required. This also applies to freelance translator / translation agency relationships.

One of the most difficult problems is that translation has become a cost-led business. A customer sees only the end product and has little knowledge of what is involved in its provision. It is seldom that the customer has the ability or facilities for checking the quality of a translation. A translator who has, say, 20 years experience is unlikely to be offered a higher translation rate than a newly-qualified translator although there are exceptions. The customer needs to be aware that the least expensive translation is not likely to be the best quality translation.

A book on international business[4] suggests that firms who require translation of important documentation should thoroughly investigate any potential translator and offers a number of points to be covered during the candidate's interview. While this sentiment is laudable, the time constraints normally demanded by a customer for a translation's production preclude this. The author also suggests a number of points to be considered during the candidate's interview including *'Does the translator have a staff or access to experts in various fields (i.e. law)?'* [sic]. The reverse is normally the case and most translators work on their own but confer with colleagues or clients when required.

While the author provides some good examples of blunders which most professional and experienced translators are aware of, he has little awareness of the constraints under which most translators work. He also suggests back-translation as a means of quality control. In all my years as a translator I have been asked to make back translations of other translators' work by only a few customers.

What to do?

Good customer relations are based on dialogue and engagement and translation needs to be an integral part of the document engineering process. Buyers of translation services need to be made aware of what skills are required to produce a good translation and involve the translator as early as possible.

The dangers of price pressure – the vicious circle

While every business endeavours to remain competitive there is a serious risk that students will look at what can be earned as a translator and think *'Why should I spend five years at university to gain an MA in translation when the fees I can hope to earn as a translator are pitifully low by comparison with other professions and jobs?'* There is already evidence that fewer students are enrolling in translation courses and that universities are diversifying to make up for the shortfall caused by the decline in the number of students of translation.

4. Ricks, D.A. (1999) *Blunders in International Business*. Blackwell Publishers Ltd, Oxford.

While price pressure reigns it is invariably the translator who offers the lowest price who will be offered the job. While there are good translators who will accept low prices the risk is that customers will accept lower prices from less qualified and less experience translators. A further risk is that the customer has no way of assessing the quality of a translation unless it is subjected to further checking. The most dangerous risk is that the end user will look at the translated documentation and consider it a reflection of the goods or services being offered. Anticipated sales will not materialise and the vendor will be unaware that the quality of the product/service documentation is the weakest link.

All of us have made jokes about the poor quality of translations in instruction leaflets that are supplied with products. While this may be a source of amusement, the result is that the customer is unable to use the product appropriately and this can result in additional costs to deal with warranty and other issues. This applies not only to translations but poor quality documentation in general. Quite often the documentation is produced in a hurry once a product or service is ready to market. This should not be case since the documentation should be written in parallel with product or service development.

Benchmarking, differentiation and best practice

What is benchmarking?

Benchmarking is a systematic process of comparing and measuring the performance of your key business activities over time and using lessons learned from your experiences to make targeted improvements and strive towards excellence.

Types of benchmarking

Internal – a comparison of internal operations.
Competitive – a comparison against a specific competitor for the product, service or function of interest.
Generic – a comparison of business functions or processes that are the same, regardless of industry or country.

Why benchmark?

1.　You want to improve (uphold your reputation).
2.　Your competitors are doing it.
3.　Your customers are demanding it.
4.　It costs six times more to win a new customer than retain one.
5.　It will show that you are interested in your customers – be pro-active.

6. ISO 9001:2000 puts customer satisfaction at the centre of its focus. Monitoring your performance to show continuous improvement meets the needs of the new quality standard.

How can your organisation differentiate itself from the competition?

In an increasingly competitive environment, an organisation needs to differentiate itself from other services providers if it is going to succeed. The following table lists the resources you may have at your disposal and compares these with what the competition has to offer.

Differentiating factors	What the competition offers	In what way(s) are you different?
Physical resources – Office premises	Competing companies all have offices.	These are not always important since customers seldom visit their suppliers. We should however encourage customers to visit us and see how we operate. This could be a strong differentiating factor.
Physical resources – Information technology	Competing companies all have technology resources.	You are probably no different from most of the competition. The cost of extending your range of hardware and software to meet some demands is difficult to justify. Do you get the software to meet a perceived need or wait until the customer 'demands' that you get the software?
Pricing	All companies try to be competitive on price	Getting into a price war is a losing strategy. If you can differentiate your organisation in a manner that is perceived to be beneficial by the customer then pricing is less sensitive.
Reputation	Well-established companies offer a solid reputation.	You probably have a good reputation among your existing customers and suppliers otherwise you would not remain in business. You need to make sure that potential customers are fully aware of this. Promote the unique features of your reputation by applying the 'So what?' test.
Project and quality management	Most agencies and companies offer this facility	You probably have anecdotal proof of your ability to manage large projects as well as endorsements from a number of significant customers – these should be used in promotion. Consider working towards accreditation to ISO 9001:2000 if you have not achieved this already. An organisation may be automatically excluded by some potential customers if it cannot provide evidence of recognised accreditation.

Differentiating factors	What the competition offers	In what way(s) are you different?
Human resources	All companies have human resources.	Every individual is different and thus no other company has the unique mix of human resources that your organisation has. Your organisation needs promote its strengths and develop these resources to generate a powerful competitive advantage.

Investors in People

One of the long-term objectives in a business plan would be to consider an analysis of the appropriateness and potential benefits of gaining accreditation according to 'Investors in People'. Since any translation services provider is a skills-based enterprise it is entirely appropriate that staff be offered appropriate training and coaching so that they can perform efficiently. It is also important that staff feel a sense of achievement and satisfaction with what they do.

Once your organisation has achieved accreditation to ISO 9001:2000 it seems appropriate to embark on a programme for Investors in People. An outline structure for this is as follows.

This program would extend over a period of 12–15 months and is in four phases:

Phase 1 – Commitment

This is a commitment from management to develop the employees so that business objectives can be achieved.

- There must be a commitment from management to develop and train employees. This commitment must be communicated effectively throughout the organisation.
- Employees at all level are aware of the broad aims of the organisation.
- The organisation considers what employees at all levels will contribute to the success of the organisation, and communicates this to them.

Phase 2 – Production of an action plan

An Investor in People organisation regularly reviews needs and plans the training and development of all its employees not just translators but also support staff.

- A flexible written plan sets out the organisation's goals and targets.
- The plan identifies the organisation's training and development needs, and specifies what actions will be taken to meet these demands.

- Training and development needs are regularly reviewed against goals and targets at the organisation, team and individual level.
- The plan identifies the resources that will be used to meet training and development needs.
- Responsibility for training and developing employees is clearly identified and understood throughout the organisation, starting at the top.
- Objectives are set for training and development actions at the organisation, team and individual level.
- Where appropriate, training and development objectives are linked to external standards such as NVQs.

Phase 3 – Implementation

An Investor in People company takes action to train and develop individuals as they are recruited and throughout their employment.

All new employees are introduced effectively to the organisation. All employees are given the training and development they need to do that job.

- Managers must be effective in carrying out their responsibilities for training and developing employees.
- Managers are actively involved in supporting employees to meet their training and development needs.
- All employees are aware of the training and development opportunities that are open to them.
- All employees are encouraged to help identify and meet their job-related training and development needs.
- Measures are implemented to meet the training and development needs of individuals, teams and the organisation.

Phase 4 – Assessment

An Investor in People company evaluates the investment in training and development to assess achievement and improve future effectiveness.

- The organisation evaluates the impact of training and development measures on knowledge skills and attitude.
- The organisation evaluates the impact of training and development measures on performance.
- The organisation evaluates the contribution of training and development to the achievement of its goals and targets.

- Management understands the broad cost and benefits of training and developing people.
- Action takes place to implement improvements to training and development identified as a result of evaluation.
- Management continuing commitment to training and developing employees is demonstrated to all employees.

What are the benefits of Investor in People?

Investor in People status brings public recognition for real achievements measured against a rigorous National Standard. Being an Investor in People sends a strong signal to customers, suppliers, employees and stakeholders. Recognised organisations attract the best quality job applicants. Achieving the Standard may also provide a reason for customers to prefer your organisation as a services provider.

Through improved performance, an Investor in People company develops a competitive edge which goes a long way to securing future profitability and prosperity.

To my knowledge, very few translation companies yet have Investor in People recognition. This, together with ISO 9002 accreditation, could be a very powerful tool in differentiating ourselves from the competition.

What are the arguments against embarking on an Investor in People programme?

We can't afford the time or money	The same argument could be directed at an ISO 9001 programme. But, having implemented ISO 9001 it is unlikely that the organisation would like to revert to the way it worked before accreditation.
Isn't ISO 9001 enough?	Investor in People significantly improves the results of quality programmes and adds considerable value to ISO 9001. By meeting the standard we would be putting in place processes which are key to implementing the European Quality Model.
Don't we have enough procedures?	Investor in People is about results. Significant commercial benefits may be gained by companies which achieve the standard. These benefits begin to appear while working towards becoming an Investor in People.

9 Your Exit Strategy

Probably the last think on your mind when starting a business is how you are going to plan your exit. This may come about for a number of reasons the most important of which are planning your retirement and ensuring a satisfactory pension and other benefits, responding to an unsolicited offer to buy your company or merging it with a competitor.

Let me say before I go any further that I am not in any way a financial advisor. I can speak only on the basis of my own experience of developing a business from a one-man band to a translation company with 15 employees and then selling it in response to an unsolicited offer. You should seek the advice of your financial advisor since rules and regulations change from time to time and what is valid at the moment may not necessarily apply at some date in the future.

Planned retirement

This assumes that you are the majority shareholder in your business and can therefore make whatever decision you choose. You may have given small number of shares in your company to reward key employees and these will need to be considered when they either leave the company or you sell the company and their shares need to be purchased. The level at which you can discuss this depends on the sensitivity of the information.

As a director of a company you can set up a director's pension scheme into which you make regular payments. This has the advantage that contributions are not taxed when paid in and you will probably pay tax at a lower rate when you start to draw your pension. How you structure this needs to be discussed with your financial advisor. In my case I purchased an endowment using my pension fund which allowed me to take a lump sum of 25% of the fund tax free and then started to draw a very small pension which allowed me to cut back on work commitments. The date at which I decide to retire fully is my choice, providing what I deliver is satisfactory, and the longer I decide to work the greater the monthly pension I can enjoy. Everything depends of course on the size of the pension fund you have managed to build up.

The issue of capital gains tax on the sale of the business needs to be considered. Retirement relief is available to individuals who have attained the age of 50 at the time of disposal. Relief can be granted at an earlier age if somebody retires as a consequence of serious ill health. A person needs to have worked in the business for 10 years to obtain full relief. Relief is reduced on a pro-rata basis for shorter periods. Other conditions apply so consult your advisor for current information.

Selling your business

Grooming your business for sale

Whether you advertise your business for sale or your respond to an unsolicited offer will have a considerable impact on your selling strategy. You can groom your company so that it looks at its best when the time comes to sell. For this you need to plan way in advance if you are going to get the biggest cheque and the best deal. Businesses seldom produce good profits over long period especially when making major investments that may not realise any dividends until some time in the future. Make sure your business is running fit and lean. Cut back on all expenditure that cannot be justified or is dubious in any way. Consider how you can make your company look the most attractive to any prospective purchaser. Your accounts should be structured to show maximum profits rather than trying to reduce paper profits to mitigate any tax liability.

Any prospective purchaser and his advisors will go through your books with a very fine-tooth comb. Planning your sale in advance allows you to ensure that all your paperwork and accounts are up to date. You might consider re-registering the company as a Plc – after all it is your corporate image that is important. This applies not only to any potential buyers but other people and organisations you deal with.

There are so many issues you need to consider, not least what might happen to the people who are employed in the business. You can coldly consider that once you have sold the business then what happens to it afterwards is no business of yours since you no longer own the company. Verbal promises to retain the structure as it is are seldom kept and any regrets you have after having sold the business are something you have to live with. You have to consider whether you want to remain involved in a part-time basis or make a clean break.

The most important consideration is to appoint an advisor who can act as your intermediary. He will need to have the appropriate connections and a good track record. Don't just accept the first advisor who presents himself. Make an appointment to meet potential advisors at their premises. Make sure you are dealing with the person who will act on you behalf. You will need to have confidence in your advisor since he will be party to very confidential business and private information. Question him about his experience. He should be professionally qualified as an accountant or solicitor. If he is a solicitor he should be qualified in corporate law. Fortunately I had a very good advisor when I sold my business. I asked the company's solicitor to deal with the legal aspects of the sale but it very quickly became apparent that he had little experience in such matters and was literally carried by my advisor. I asked the solicitor for a quote in advance but his final bill came to twice the amount! I found out about the amount once the profit from the sale of the business (after fees paid to the advisor, the accountants and the solicitor had been deducted) had been completed. I got the feeling that the solicitor was learning the process at my expense. To be properly protected make sure you engage an experience corporate lawyer.

If and when you advertise your business for sale you need to maintain tight-lipped security. Any responses to your advertisement will include genuine enquiries and well as those from time-wasters, people with no money, those who would like to capitalise on the deal and, not least, from competitors. Once somebody in the company becomes aware about a potential sale there can be disastrous consequences, usually as a response to pure speculation, such as your best people thinking the company is on the way out and applying for jobs elsewhere. Obvious purchasers are competitors. This can be good and bad since they know the profession and its strengths and weakness. It is probably that principal asset is your customer database and they will be looking at how the purchase can add value to their own business.

You will need to put together a presentation of your company in the form of a prospectus or Information Memorandum. This should provide answers to any questions a prospective purchase might pose and provide your advisor (who is probably your intermediary) with right information so that he can make the best presentation of you business. This should include history and background (including your unique selling points), sales, operations, premises, management and staff, and financial information.

Any potential buyer will need to perform what is referred to as due diligence. This comprises a detailed investigation into your business and will look at the company's records to support its value and whether there are issues that have been concealed. This investigation may include reports from solicitors and accountants. Obviously the diligence process should be covered by confidentiality undertakings and supported by warranties.

Price

There is no specific formula for calculating the price of a business since it is based on so many intangibles. A potential buyer will be looking for an acceptable rate of return on his investment while the seller will be looking for the best deal possible. The assets of the business are obviously important as are an exclusive position in the market. Cashflow is also important. A business whose cashflow is healthy is more desirable than one that is cash-hungry and has a hard time yielding surpluses. Turnover is vanity, profit is sanity whereas money in the bank is reality!

Dependence on one or two major customers is a weakness. Although it is gratifying to win major contracts it is necessary to consider vulnerability and what would happen if that contract came to an end or was cancelled for some reason. The company's database of freelance translators is certainly an asset but each of the translators on the database probably works for at least a dozen other agencies – including the one that is considering buying you business.

Translation is a secretive profession and it is almost impossible to make comparisons as you would if you were buying a house or a car. Some people use what is referred to as the price earnings ratio or P/E ratio. This compares the current market price of a share with the earnings (after corporation tax) of that share. Several ratios are used in accounting and using just one ratio does not give a clear picture. Often the value of a company is what a buyer is prepared to pay for it. This takes no account of the company's potential nor its profit history.

Though you may not have any immediate intention of selling your business, it is worth the effort to be prepared since a unique opportunity may present itself through an unsolicited approach from a potential buyer. Try and view your company from the viewpoint of a potential buyer and carry out a critical SWOT analysis. This may uncover simple measures whose implementation could vastly enhance the attractiveness of your business.

10 References

Organisations for translation companies

The principal organisations in the United Kingdom for translators and translation companies are:

Association of Translation Companies

The Association of Translation Companies was formed in 1976 by a group of leading translation companies in Britain, making it one of the oldest organisations representing the interests of translation companies in the world.

Over the years the Association has expanded its horizons and attracted members from around the world. For those seeking to source translations, the Association acts as an impartial clearing house guiding them to those members most suited to help them.

ATC members must carry professional indemnity insurance cover and adhere to an agreed Code of Professional Conduct, which has now become the profession's standard. In cases of dispute between a client and a translation company, whether it is a member or not, the Association offers an independent arbitration service.

Because the Association represents the translation company sector of the profession, it can talk with authority to legislators about matters affecting the translation industry. The ATC is a founding member of the European Union of Association of Translation Companies – a pan-European grouping of translation company associations.

The Association's web address is: www.atc.org.uk.

The Institute of Linguists

While the Institute of Linguists does not accept corporate members, it is appropriate to mention one of its divisions – the Business, Professions and Government Division.

The strength of the division lies in its diversity, which in itself represents a strategic challenge to the committee behind it!

The members of the Division may use their languages as a primary or secondary function, regularly or intermittently, with specialised or general terminology, but largely in support of, or complementary to, another discipline within the sphere of commerce and industry.

For instance, the current divisional management committee includes a marine biologist, a business development manager for a steel company, translators and small business advisors – but none of the committee could perform these functions with the same degree of professionalism without the language skills which give them the 'edge'.

Mission statements may now be considered 'old hat', but the Business, Professions and Government Division considers its objectives to be the following:

To provide networking opportunities for its members supported by informative and stimulating events.

To promote the value of language skills and to enhance the respect accorded to linguists within the context of industry and commerce.

To create and maintain awareness within the industrial/commercial world of the benefits of cross-cultural communication.

One of our new initiatives is to welcome and inform new divisional members, and to seek their views about events or information which would benefit them.

This is done by means of a welcome pack and questionnaire, to be followed up by a programme of 'regional socials' for new and existing divisional members to provide a networking platform in a pleasant and sociable atmosphere.

A recent survey of new divisional members indicated that the main motivation for joining the division was 'business/industry-related events', followed by 'networking with colleagues' and 'language-related events'. The majority of new members who responded worked in the areas designated 'industry/services sector: support role' and 'translation/interpreting', which for the majority of Business, Professions and Government Division members represents part of their varied duties to a greater or lesser extent. English was listed as the most frequently used language at work, followed by German, French – no surprises there – but then a little further down the list came Chinese, Russian and more specifically Cantonese and Mandarin.

The Institute of Translation & Interpreting

The Institute of Translation & Interpreting was founded in 1986 as the only independent professional association of practising translators and interpreters in the United Kingdom. It is now one of the primary sources of information on these services to government, industry, the media and the general public. With its aim of promoting the highest standards in the profession, ITI serves as a meeting place for all those who understand the importance of translation and interpreting to the economy and society, particularly with the expansion of a single European market of over forty languages and the growth of worldwide communications. ITI offers guidance to those entering the profession and advice not only to those who offer language services but also to their customers.

ITI has a large and growing international membership of translators and interpreters, not just in the United Kingdom but also in continental Europe and other countries where English is commonly used. Different levels of membership are on offer to suit translators and interpreters with varying amounts of experience, from newcomers to the industry to experienced professionals.

Members are required to abide by the Institute's professional code of conduct. They will be expected to subscribe to ITI's aims and are encouraged to take an active part in its life and events. Corporate membership is also open to educational, commercial and government bodies as well as translation companies.

The Institute's web address is www.iti.org.

Other relevant organisations

The Institute of Scientific and Technical Communicators

The ISTC is the largest UK body representing professional communicators and information designers and has been established for more than 50 years.

Its objective is to improve standards for communication of the scientific and technical information supporting services and business. Its vision is for professional communicators to provide information to enable a user to use a product or service safely and efficiently.

The Institute's web address is www.istc.org.uk.

European Union of Associations of Translation Companies

The EUATC is an international organisation and the only one of its kind in Europe representing quality-oriented translation companies. It was established in 1994 and its members are national associations of translation companies.

Membership is not restricted to EU member states. In fact, the EUATC welcomes new members from other European countries.

All the member associations appoint two representatives to attend EUATC meetings. The office of President is occupied for a term of two years and rotates among the members.

As a truly international organisation the EUATC is a forum for translation businesses, enabling them to speak with a united voice and providing them with a lobby on issues affecting the translation industry. Resolutions are implemented swiftly and efficiently, with meetings taking place at least twice a year.

The EUATC is a body which is recognised by the European Commission in Brussels. As a major opinion leader it participates in influencing European policy and decision-making and is consulted by key international institutions. One of the current projects is to create a unified, Europe-wide quality standard for translation companies.

The EUATC provides a platform for members on which they can address issues involving the translation industry as a whole. It has a Training Committee which looks after professional translator training and encourages the efficient use of state-of-the-art translation tools.

It takes a proactive approach to promoting the translation process across Europe and is committed to developing Europe-wide quality standards and good translation practice. The members of the EUATC work together in order to achieve common goals and derive mutual benefit from sharing important information.

The Union's web address is www.euatc.org.

LISA

Founded in 1990, LISA is the premier non-profit organization for the GILT (Globalization, Internationalization, Localization, and Translation) business community. Over 400 leading IT manufacturers and services providers, along with industry professionals representing corporations with an international business focus, have helped establish LISA's best practice guidelines and language-technology standards for enterprise globalization. It's the organization to join when you're serious about international business.

Who Can Join? Any legal or natural person, association, or organization working directly or indirectly in the facilitation of enterprise globalization and/or multilingual information management in relation to global business transactions, including, but not limited to, automated workflow technologies, product and services internationalization, localization, translation, industry consultation, and related business practices.

LISA's web address is www.lisa.org.

FIT

The FIT is a worldwide body for translation associations and membership excludes commercial organisations. However, since many translation associations accept corporate members themselves it could be useful to approach these associations if you plan to establish a strong presence in another country.

The FIT's website is www.fit-ift.org.

11 Reading List

Adams, A. (2000) *Law for Business Students*. Pearson Education Limited, Harlow.

Cava, R. (1990) *Dealing with Difficult People*. Judy Piatkus (Publishers) Ltd, London.

Donovan, P. and Samler, P. (1994) *Delighting Customers*. Chapman and Hall, London.

Johnson, G. and Scholes, K. (1993) *Exploring Corporate Strategy – Text and Cases*. Prentice Hall Europe, Hemel Hempstead.

Mole, J. (1995) *Mind your Manners – Managing Business Cultures in Europe*. Nicholas Brealey Publishing, London.

Morley, G. (1999) *How to Sell Your Business and Live Happily Ever After*. Management Books 2000 Ltd., Chalford.

Samuelsson-Brown, G.F. (2004) *A Practical Guide for Translators*, 4th Edition. Multilingual Matters, Clevedon.

Trompenaars, F. and Hampden-Turner, C. (2002) *Riding the Waves of Culture – Understanding Cultural Diversity in Business*. Nicholas Brealey, London.

Williams, S. (1999) *Small Business Guide*. Penguin Books, London (contains a comprehensive list of further reading).

12 Appendices

Appendix 1 – Documented standards relevant to translation

BS 4755:1971

Specification for the presentation of translations.

BS 5261 Part 2

The standard provides a specification for typographic requirements, marks for copy preparation and proof correction, proofing procedure.

DIN 2345

The DIN 2345 standard was published by the German Institute for Standardization in 1998. This standard contains different conditions for concluding contracts between translators and clients. Among the issues the standard considers are:

1) The original (or source) text
2) Choosing the translator
3) Setting up a contract between client and translator
4) Target text
5) Proofreading

ISO 2384:1977

The standard sets out rules to ensure that translations are presented in a standard form which will simplify their use by different categories of user. Applies to the translation of all documents, whether the translation is complete, partial or abridged. Four types of translation are discussed.

UNI 10574:1995

Definition of services and activities of translation and interpreting enterprises

European Translation Standard

This standard is currently under review.

Appendix 2 – Model of a job interview record

XYZ Translations Limited
JOB INTERVIEW RECORD

Name of applicant: . . . .

Position applied for: . . . .

Interviewer: . . . .

Date of interview: . . . .

Purpose

It is important that we select and appoint the most appropriate candidate with the relevant formal qualifications, skills and experience for any new staff position or to fill a position that becomes vacant. Sufficient details must be entered on this record for this purpose, and to identify initial training that may be needed to meet corporate objectives.

Interview question	Interviewer's notes
Tell me about the jobs you have listed on your CV that could be relevant to this position.	
What were the reasons for leaving your present job (last job)?	
What interests you about this job?	
What do consider to be your strengths and limitations?	
How would you deal with a difficult customer?	
How would you describe yourself? Calm, impatient, assertive, etc.	

Interview question	Interviewer's notes
What do you consider to be the most important aspects to you about a job and why?	
What software do you have skills in?	
How do you see your own set of skills and competence developing?	
Tell me what you understand by quality management?	
Other job-specific questions based on job description	

Personal attributes and inter-personal skills (observations made by the interviewer)

Appearance and dress	
Spoken communication	
Body language	
Attitude	
What can the candidate offer in addition to basic skills required?	

General notes (include details of any training that may be needed)

Additional notes compiled after the interview candidate has left

(The interviewer should read through the above notes, reflect on the interview and then make additional notes as required.)

Result of interview

Reject candidate ❏   Short-list for further consideration ❏   Offer position to this candidate ❏

Signature of person conducting the interview

. . . .

When this Interview Assessment Form is completed it is filed in the locked personnel records.

Office use only

Notes to be filed for reference?	Yes	❏
	No	❏

Appendix 3 – Model for compiling staff regulations

Introductory note

The following is provided as a guide only and should not be considered a legal document. It needs to be modified to suit the individual organisation.

Note that government and other regulations change over time. These regulations were correct at the time of compilation but should be revised to comply with current regulations.

XYZ Translation Services Ltd.
Staff Regulations

These regulations were originally drawn up after having consulted the Chairman of the Professional Standards Committee of the Institute of Translation and Interpreting. Opinion has also been sought from other translation companies to determine what is currently accepted practice within the profession. ACAS was also consulted when formulating the disciplinary procedure.

The use of the masculine form of the third person is purely a practical consideration – no gender discrimination is intended or implied. These regulations apply equally to the feminine as to the masculine third person.

Date of issue: . . . .

Welcome to XYZ Translations Ltd.
We hope that your employment with the company will be long, mutually-rewarding and satisfying. We also hope that you will quickly feel at home, and an integral and valued part of our very professional team.

XYZ's reputation
XYZ has an excellent reputation, not only in the United Kingdom but also internationally. XYZ probably has an excellent team of translators in the United Kingdom supplemented with an extensive database of freelance languages. This team is augmented with in-house translators working with other languages, and other staff who provide operations management and administration support.

Good teamwork depends on a high degree of give-and-take between all those involved. Working together and supporting each other provides the foundation for our continued success, and provides benefit for all those involved.

XYZ offers strong support to the translation profession, not only through its policy of staff skills development but also through its external involvement.

General regulations

In addition to your contract of employment and any additional terms contained in your offer of employment, there are a number of rules of principle that apply to all members of staff. Legislation also requires the company to state the disciplinary and grievance procedures in detail. Nevertheless we sincerely hope that neither will ever be required.

These rules may be vary from time to time as matters are raised that require policy decisions. Although the opinion of staff members may be sought in this connection, the employer has the final right of decision.

There is always scope for improvement in working methods in terms of time, efficiency and cost saving. Suggestions are always welcome.

If you have any questions about these staff regulations, or any other aspects that 'formalise' your work, please feel free to discuss them with me at anytime.

Working hours

XYZ operates a 35-hour working week. Core working hours are between 09.00 and 17.00, Monday to Friday, with one hour for lunch at a convenient time between 12.00 and 14.00 hrs. Exceptions to the latter may be necessary on occasions, but not as a matter of regular practice, to comply with customer requirements or special circumstances and must be approved by the Commercial Director.

All staff are required to sign in or out when arriving at or leaving XYZ's premises so that all staff can be accounted for if the building needs to the evacuated in the event of emergency.

Staff are discouraged from eating breakfast during working hours at their desk on arrival at work. Staff must not take their lunch at their desk and then an additional hour for lunch. We need to consider the professional image we project to visitors. The conference room can be used for checking if available.

These hours are implemented for several important reasons. Consider what would happen if a member of staff had an accident or became ill and nobody were able to provide assistance.

The regulations have been compiled for additional reasons:

- to harmonise with standard commercial practice,
- to harmonise working hours and so that resources can be better controlled and utilised,
- to enhance security and reduce the vulnerability of individuals being the office alone in the event of an intruder making an unauthorised entry.

Flexible working hours will be permitted between 08.00 and 18.00 hours subject to approval by the Managing Director. Designated staff will ensure telephone coverage during the lunch hour.

Personal development

XYZ will provide training so that an individual member of staff can perform his or her work satisfactorily and efficiently. Further details are found in the Investors in People portfolio. Training requirements are identified during discussions between line managers and staff during appraisals and quarterly reviews. XYZ will reimburse the cost of additional personal development subject to certain criteria. Personal development includes, but is not limited to, attending approved further education and applications to become a member of a professional association. The principal criteria for approval are:

- applications for reimbursement shall be made on the appropriate form and submitted to your line manager for approval. Approved applications are then submitted to the Commercial Director for payment,
- applications for membership submitted to a professional association shall be made in the name of XYZ using XYZ's address. Such fees will not be reimbursed if a private address and telephone number are given,
- reimbursement is conditional on XYZ deriving commercial benefit from an applicant's personal development or membership of a professional association,
- that the training budget drawn up at the beginning of the year by your line manager for your department has sufficient funds.

Secrecy declaration and covenant
On appointment, staff shall give an undertaking in writing to observe strict secrecy with regard to information concerning the company and its customers which they may obtain knowledge during the course of their employment.

Because of the type of work we do, all members of staff are required to undergo government clearance.

Under no circumstances may any information about XYZ or its customers that is not in the public domain be made available to anybody outside the company. All of us in the company are bound by non-disclosure agreements with customers.

The consequences of any breach of such agreements could have a devastating effect on the company's future. At best we would lose the customer and could suffer legal consequences of any such breach. At worst, we could be sued and put out of business.

Holidays
Your terms and conditions of employment state your individual entitlement. Note that it is XYZ's policy to close the office between Christmas and New Year and staff are therefore advised to save leave for this period. Unpaid leave will be permitted for this period subject to approval.

All leave applications shall be submitted to your line manager for approval. Your line manager will then notify the Commercial Director who will enter the details on your leave record.

The standard entitlement for the full first year of employment is XX days paid holiday plus paid public holidays. The company's financial year is the same as the calendar year and, if you join the company some way through the year, your entitlement for that year will be calculated *pro rata*.

The standard holiday entitlement will be increased to XX days after two years' service followed by an increment of one day for each subsequent year of service up to a maximum of XX days. The Managing Director has the discretion to make individual awards outside this framework.

Unpaid leave will be granted providing this is approved by your line manager and does not conflict with scheduled work. Compassionate leave will granted at the discretion of your line manager.

If you decide to leave the company part way through the calendar year and you have used more than your *pro rata* entitlement for that part of the year you have worked, your final salary will be adjusted to take this into account.

Sickness leave and benefits
The company recognises the provision for payment of sickness benefit in accordance with the relevant sections of current national insurance legislation.

Maternity leave and benefits
The company recognises the provision for payment of maternity benefits in accordance with the relevant sections of current employment legislation.

Health and safety at work
The company recognises and accepts its responsibility as an employer for providing a safe and healthy place of work for its employees and will take all practical steps to meet this responsibility.

It is the duty of each individual employee whilst at work to bring to the attention of management any hazards that, in his view, need to be rectified.

Any employee with specific responsibilities for aspects of health and safety must ensure that his responsibilities are properly delegated in his absence.

A member of staff has been appointed to provide first aid.

Personal telephone calls
The company accepts that there is the need, on occasions, for personal calls to be made from the office using XYZ's telephones. Such calls must be kept to a minimum.

The use of personal mobile phones during working hours should be limited.

Dress and conduct
Staff are expected to dress and conduct themselves in the manner that befits a member of a professional service provider whenever they are at the office or otherwise identified as representing the company.

No smoking policy
XYZ's premises and the office building we occupy are designated a non-smoking area and no provision is made for smokers inside the building. This applies equally to visitors.

Security of information
Events have shown the disruption a 'harmless' virus can cause and how much staff time can be wasted and production time lost. The company endeavours to take the necessary steps to ensure that

it operates legitimately and it has the required number of software licenses.

Under no circumstances may any disk or tape be brought into the company, or taken out of the company, without the permission of the Managing Director. This applies to disks and tapes with text, graphics or other files, and company software. As a company director, the Managing Director could face a substantial fine or a prison sentence of two years if he permits the unauthorised use of company software licenses.

Unauthorised use of company information, documentation, computer disks or tapes, or the company's electronic mail system to receive or transmit confidential information about the company, its intellectual property or its customers will result in immediate dismissal.

Contravention of this regulation will be considered a disciplinary matter.

File backups
The computer network server is used to make copies of all work in progress or completed. All staff are required to make regular backups of work in progress on the server in accordance with the ISO 9001:2000 instruction. Backups are made on a daily basis and taken off-site.

Any work that is lost through not making the required backup shall be re-done in the erring person's time or the relevant cost deducted from the respective member of staff's salary.

Working to ISO 9001:2000
All staff are expected to work to maintain the level of quality that relates to this

standard. The current copy of XYZ's Quality Manual is available in the library.

Private enterprise
While the company cannot prevent any member of staff engaging in other commercial activities outside contracted working hours, taking on freelance work during office hours or using the company's facilities for private enterprise is not permitted.

As a consequence, any communication with private customers shall be kept strictly private and shall not be conducted during working hours using a private mobile phone, the company's telephone, fax, modem, email, or copying facilities.

Disciplinary procedure
The company requires all employees to conduct themselves in accordance with its rules and procedures and to perform their work to a satisfactory standard in order to maintain an efficient and successful business. If these rules are contravened, or satisfactory standards of performance are not maintained, formal disciplinary action may be taken.

The procedure exists to deal with misconduct which covers:

- Failure to achieve a proper standard in the performance of the employee's job, e.g. persistent lapses in administrative control.
- Persistent minor misconduct and breach of terms of employment. Examples of this might be persistent lateness for work, persistent use of bad language, the failure to notify

the company of reasons for absence, or to produce a medical certificate promptly in case of sickness that extends beyond seven days.

- Gross misconduct and major breaches of terms and conditions of employment. Whilst it is not possible to specify all types of behaviour that could constitute misconduct, some examples are gross insubordination, assault, misuse of company property, and involvement of the company's name in fraudulent or scandalous behaviour.
- No form of bullying will be tolerated at XYZ. Bullying is defined as regular and persistent physical or psychological harassment involving criticism and humiliation. It undermines the confidence of the victim and leads to lower performance. At worst it can cause depression and an inability to do the job for which the victim is employed.

    When people are repeatedly and aggressively criticised they feel they cannot do anything right. Such behaviour destroys teamwork, commitment and morale.

Everybody at XYZ should work towards achieving a culture where people treat each other with courtesy and respect.

Principles of operation
The procedure is based on the following principles:

- There will be no dismissal for the first breach of discipline except in the case of gross misconduct, where immediate dismissal may result.
- There shall be provision for an employee to be accompanied by a colleague at any disciplinary interview.
- There shall be provision for a right of appeal to a level of management not previously involved.

The company hopes that this procedure will never need be applied to any of its employees. It is a requirement of employment legislation to explain this procedure in detail.

To ensure that disciplinary matters are dealt with in an impartial and fair manner, and that any disciplinary action taken is clearly understood, the following procedure will apply.

Where it is considered that there has been breach of discipline, the individual will be interviewed by his manager. The individual will be given the opportunity to have a colleague present if he wishes. The individual must be given the opportunity to state his case before any decision is made on the disciplinary action to be taken.

Depending on the seriousness of the breach, if the manager decides that disciplinary action is needed, he will take one of four courses, as follows:

- Deliver a verbal warning. This normally covers minor breaches such as lateness, persistent sickness, and poor work performance. A reasonable specified period of time should be given for the correction of performance or behaviour. A note of this should be made and placed on the individual's file.

- Deliver a first written warning. This would cover a more serious breach or an accumulation of minor breaches where verbal warnings had been given to no avail.
- Deliver a final written warning. This will normally be given where no improvement has followed from a written warning but may also be given for a first offence if it is of a very serious nature.

Dismissal

This may occur if no improvement has been achieved after the above procedure has been carried out. It may also occur in cases of gross misconduct.

Employees cannot be dismissed before an investigation has been carried out.

Suspension

In the case of suspected gross misconduct or a major breach of terms and conditions, an employee may be suspended pending investigation and dismissal may result.

The right to appeal

At all stages, the employee must be told that he has the right to appeal against any disciplinary action taken against him. Appeals must be submitted, in writing to the Managing Director, within two days of a verbal warning having been given, or within two days of receipt of a written warning or letter confirming dismissal. The Managing Director will hear the appeal and decide the case as impartially as possible. The decision of the Managing Director is final.

Grievance procedure

An employee with a grievance relating to his employment should, in the first instance, discuss the matter with the person to whom he is immediately responsible.

If the matter is not settled at this stage, the employee should take up his grievance with the Managing Director, whose decision is final.

At all stages of the procedure, the employee may be accompanied by a colleague if he so wishes.

At each stage where there has been failure to resolve a grievance, a statement in writing recording the outcome that stage of the procedure should be agreed for reference to the next stage.

Not more than five working days shall elapse between a recorded failure to resolve a grievance and its reference to the Managing Director.

The procedure is not necessarily invalidated if, for some mutually accepted reason, more than five working days elapse.

Full details of the reasons for grievance shall be recorded. If there is failure to agree, the name of the person to whom the grievance is referred shall be shown in the record.

Summary

These regulations are intended for your general guidance. Other documents exist, or may be produced, that set up the way things are done within the company. We hope that you will play an active part in their drafting and continual improvement.

Today's legislation requires the company to establish and state certain rules of the procedure in the 'people' aspects of its work.

One of the characteristics the company looks for in building its team is your ability to blend in as of full member of it. This does not mean that there will always be full agreement but it does limit the risk of serious disputes

With these regulations and your contract of employment you have all the 'formal' documentation relating to your being a member of the XYZ team. Please, always ask if you have any doubt. Please come with a suggestion if you can see any way of improving any aspect of what we do.

We exist because we have customers. It takes a long time to build up a good relationship with a customer but less than a minute to lose them forever. Despite commercial pressures, it is still values such as honesty, reliability, value for money, quality, attention to detail, and compliance with customer requirements that win in long-term.

Appendix 4 – Example of Work Order Form

WORK ORDER FORM TRANSLATIONS

GSB Consulting Ltd
Filename: C:\flg\Work Order Form P1-QE.prz
Revised 2 June 2004 / Updated 2 January 2006

Job Number:

Assignment details

Language:

Word count: _____ S/T?

Editing/proofreading

Contact (if required)

Notes:

Invoice posted to client and file transferred to ARCHIVE directory: /   /06

Customer order details

Name

P/O

Date/time received: /   /06

Ref. mat? Yes ☐ No ☐ Return? ☐

Invoice information

Word count:

Rates: Standard: SEK _____ / w

Certified: SEK _____ /w

Editing/proof, hours: _____ Rate: SEK _____ /h

Express charge: ☐ 25% ☐ 50% ☐ 100%

Certification fee

Invoice total: SEK _____ EUR

Exchange rates: £ = SEK

£ = EUR

£ equivalent: £

Delivery instructions and pre-delivery checks

Date due: /   /06 Time: _____   S/W format: W4W ☐ PowerPoint ☐ Other

Date sent: /   /06 Time: _____   Delivery method: Post? ☐ Fax? ☐ Email? ☐

Translation checks
☐ Compliance with client requirements
☐ Draft translation
☐ Queries resolved with client
☐ Check for completeness
☐ Check and revise against source document
☐ Spell check
☐ Incorporation of changes
☐ Repeat spell check
☐ 2nd check against source document
☐ Final edits & pre-del. formatting

Trados checks
(Additional checks when TRADOS is used to facilitate translation)
☐ Close all segments and file before cleaning up translation
☐ Use TRADOS Tools to clean draft translation
☐ Check formatting after cleaning
☐ Final edits and pre-delivery formatting
☐ Edit .BAK file if necessary

Proofreading and editing assignments
☐ Mark up copy of original by hand if edits cannot be tracked
☐ Track changes when file is in MS Word
☐ Re-read 1st edit and mark up or track additional changes
☐ Read edited version without mark-ups visible, run spell check
☐ Incorporate final changes and send finished marked-up copy to customer

Date/initials on completion of pre-delivery checks: /   /06

Disposal date   /   /2009

Appendix 5 – Customer complaint resolution process

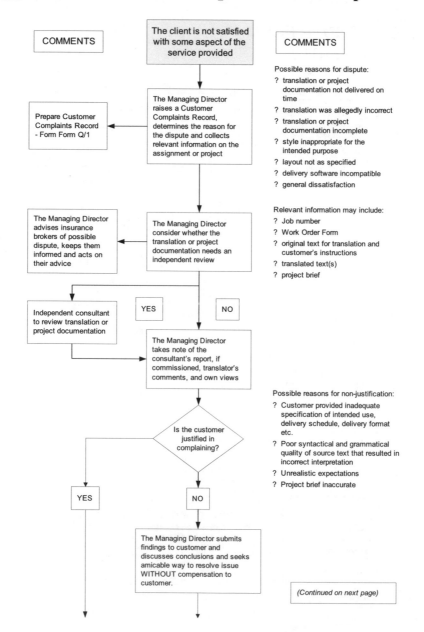

COMMENTS

The client is not satisfied with some aspect of the service provided

COMMENTS

Prepare Customer Complaints Record - Form Form Q/1

The Managing Director raises a Customer Complaints Record, determines the reason for the dispute and collects relevant information on the assignment or project

Possible reasons for dispute:
? translation or project documentation not delivered on time
? translation was allegedly incorrect
? translation or project documentation incomplete
? style inappropriate for the intended purpose
? layout not as specified
? delivery software incompatible
? general dissatisfaction

The Managing Director advises insurance brokers of possible dispute, keeps them informed and acts on their advice

The Managing Director consider whether the translation or project documentation needs an independent review

Relevant information may include:
? Job number
? Work Order Form
? original text for translation and customer's instructions
? translated text(s)
? project brief

Independent consultant to review translation or project documentation

YES

NO

The Managing Director takes note of the consultant's report, if commissioned, translator's comments, and own views

Is the customer justified in complaining?

Possible reasons for non-justification:
? Customer provided inadequate specification of intended use, delivery schedule, delivery format etc.
? Poor syntactical and grammatical quality of source text that resulted in incorrect interpretation
? Unrealistic expectations
? Project brief inaccurate

YES

NO

The Managing Director submits findings to customer and discusses conclusions and seeks amicable way to resolve issue WITHOUT compensation to customer.

(Continued on next page)

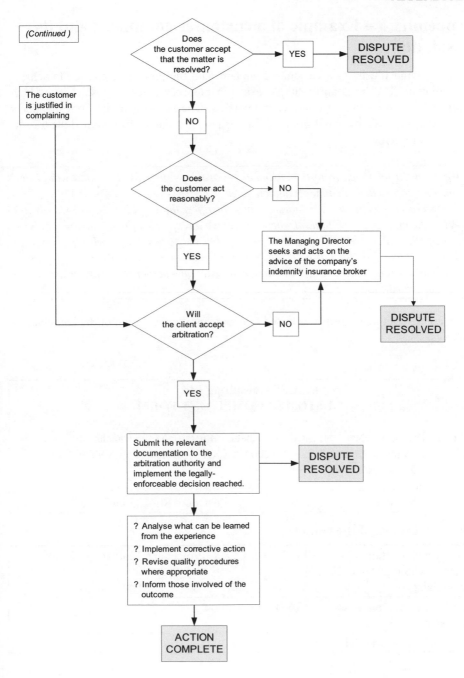

Appendix 6 – Example of a customer complaint and its resolution

The following illustrates a customer complaint and the procedure applied to achieve a resolution. This is a fairly simple example but serves its purpose. Names have been deleted to ensure customer confidentiality. The relevant initial correspondence (verbatim) received by email from the Swedish agency that commissioned the translation is given below:

> *'We received feedback from the customer regarding your ABC text, and would like your reaction to their comments and changes.*
> *They were very critical – I'm not sure how justified the criticism is, but we always review the customer's complaint when we receive a response of this kind and get back to them. Primarily we work to edit the text so that they are satisfied with the result. In the case where they have already made their own changes, we make sure to respond on what is in fact our mistake, or a matter of taste, or whether the changes are worse that our translation.'*

A customer complaint form was raised to document the resolution of the complaint as follows:

GSB Consulting Ltd
CUSTOMER COMPLAINT FORM

Customer name: (Name of the agency that commissioned the translation)
Customer reference number: (2004/XXXX)   Tel: +46 (0)8 99 99 99
Address: XXXXXXX
Town: Stockholm . . . .   County: . . . .
Country: Sweden . . . .   Postcode: SE–1234567 . . . .

Part 1 – Details of the complaint

Name and position of person who registered the complaint	XXX XXXXXX, Project and Marketing Manager
Date when complaint was registered	16 December2004
Date when job was delivered	14 December 2004

Job reference number	2004/XXXX
Description of job	Summary of ABC study
Nature of complaint	Ultra-critical comments by end customer – see email attached. Revised text produced by end customer attached for comment.
Action or compensation demanded by customer	(Agency) requested a response to end customer's complaints.
Name of person(s) who performed the work	GSB
Project manager	GSB
Immediate action taken to assist customer or alleviate problem	3-page report shows that end customer had significantly changed the text compared with the original source text and had introduced errors.

Part 2 – Investigation and resolution

Participants in the internal investigation	GSB
Professional indemnity insurance brokers informed?	No
Result of the internal investigation (continue on separate sheet(s) if necessary but make sure they are stapled to this record)	Complaint rejected after comprehensive analysis of end customer's proposed changes. One improvement accepted although translation was not incorrect.
Summary of the response to the customer. The letter to the customer must be signed by the Managing Director.	See attached report. Report to agency submitted by email. (*The report comprised an analysis of all changes in tabular form. The first column contained the original source text, the second column contained the customer's changes and final version, and the final column contained the translator's comments with acceptance or rejection of customer's changes plus justification for the comments*).
Compensation offered to the customer	None

Compensation sought from sub-contractor(s) where appropriate	N/A
Action approved, signature and date	16 December 2004
Action taken to prevent recurrence	No further action required. (*A complaint can often provide an opportunity for improvement. It is possible that justification for the use of particular terminology in the translation may be warranted. If I consider this to be the case, I add details of the reference literature used during the course of the translation*).
Amendment required to quality procedure or instruction?	No
Date filed by	20 December 2004

Appendix 7 – Sub-contractor record

XYZ Translations Ltd
SUB-CONTRACTOR RECORD
Name of sub-contractor: . . . .
Area(s) of expertise: . . . .
. . . .
Please provide résumé plus copies of relevant certificates and awards to support this application

Sub-contractor details

Name and address	
Telephone:	
Fax:	
Email:	
VAT number:	
Registered number:	
Charge rates:	£/1000 words . . . . £/hour . . . . £/day	Expenses/ mileage: £
Quality system:	
Formal qualifications:	
Reference 1	
Reference 2	

I hereby consent to the above customer references being contacted

Signature: . . . . Date: . . . . . .

Office use only

Date sent:	Date received:
Date references contacted:	Action:

Appendix 8 – Non-disclosure agreement

XYZ Translations Ltd
NON-DISCLOSURE AGREEMENT

Name of signatory: . . . .

Purpose

This agreement has been drawn up to ensure that members of staff or sub-contractors engaged by XYZ Translations Ltd are aware of the serious implications that could arise if confidential and restricted information were to be made available to unauthorised persons outside the company.

I, ... , confirm that whilst employed by or engaged as a sub-contractor by XYZ Translations Ltd (hereinafter referred to as XYZ), I undertake:

1. during my employment or period of contract and/or at any time for a period of one year after my employment with XYZ has ceased, not to divulge to any person or company any information relating to assignments undertaken for XYZ or any information relating to XYZ or its customers;

2. to endeavour to prevent the publication or disclosure to any other person of any information concerning the business or customers of XYZ at any time during and/or before the end of the abovementioned one-year period;

3. not to approach any known customer of XYZ either directly or indirectly during my employment or period of contract (except as part of my normal duties) or at any time for a period of one year after my employment or contract with XYZ has ceased, without written permission from XYZ; and

4. that, in that time, should any customer with whom I have previously been in touch with via XYZ contacts me directly with a view to providing translation, interpreting or any other services usually provided by XYZ, I will immediately refer the customer to XYZ and shall not undertake work for the said customer without written permission from XYZ.

Signed: . . . .
(Name in block capitals)   XXXXXXXXX
Dated: . . . .

Appendix 9 – Education and training record

XYZ Translations Ltd
EDUCATION & TRAINING RECORD

Name: . . . .
Position: . . . .
Manager: . . . .
Date originated: . . . .

Purpose

It is important that a record be kept of discussions between a manager and staff that concern training, what training needs are identified and the evaluation of training that is provided. This includes initial induction, in-house training and training provided by external training providers.

Induction checklist

This checklist is to be completed by the manager for the employee on arrival at XYZ Translations Ltd and then filed by the manager at the end of the first week. A copy of the completed and signed checklist is also given to the employee for reference.

Name of manager: . . . .

Signature of manager: . . . .

Data and intellectual property security

Induction item	Tick when completed
Virus awareness.	
Data security and backups	
Staff regulations regarding movement of data on disc and other electronic media	
Signing of a non-disclosure agreement.	

Quality management

Introduction to ISO 9001:2000	
Receipt of personal copies of appropriate ISO 9001:2000 documents plus a briefing on the procedures that are appropriate to the job.	
Briefing on principal duties and subsidiary duties.	

Assessment of training needs identified during or at the end of the probationary period

Details of training course

Details of the examination or course	
Date(s) or duration of course	
Qualification or award (e.g. BSc)	
Examining or training body	
How will this examination or course be of benefit to the company and how will it assist your personal development. (Continue on a separate sheet if necessary)	

RECORD OF CONTINUED EDUCATION AND TRAINING

Name of course	Training provider	Dates/duration of course
Result or qualification gained and NVQ level:		
Personal evaluation of the training:		
Comments by manager:		

(Continue on a separate sheet if necessary)

Index